IMMIGRANT FAITH

Immigrant Faith

Patterns of Immigrant Religion in the United States, Canada, and Western Europe

Phillip Connor

NEW YORK UNIVERSITY PRESS
New York and London

NEW YORK UNIVERSITY PRESS
New York and London
www.nyupress.org

References to Internet websites (URLs) were accurate at the time of writing.
Neither the author nor New York University Press is responsible for URLs
that may have expired or changed since the manuscript was prepared.

Library of Congress Cataloging-in-Publication Data
Connor, Phillip Carey, 1976–
Immigrant faith : patterns of immigrant religion in the United States,
Canada, and Western Europe / Phillip Connor.
pages cm   Includes bibliographical references and index.
ISBN 978-1-4798-5390-8 (hardback) — ISBN 978-1-4798-8379-0 (pb)
1. Immigrants—Religious life—United States. 2. Immigrants—Religious life—Canada.
3. Immigrants—Religious life—Europe, Western. 4. United States—Emigration and
immigration—Religious aspects. 5. Canada—Emigration and immigration—Religious
aspects. 6. Europe, Western—Emigration and immigration—Religious aspects.
7. United States—Social conditions—21st century. 8. Canada—Social conditions—
21st century. 9. Europe, Western—Social conditions—21st century. I. Title.
BL625.9.I55C66   2014
200.86'912—dc23   2014011584

New York University Press books are printed on acid-free paper,
and their binding materials are chosen for strength and durability.
We strive to use environmentally responsible suppliers and materials
to the greatest extent possible in publishing our books.

Manufactured in the United States of America

10 9 8 7 6 5 4 3 2 1

Also available as an ebook

To my immigrant friends, near and far

CONTENTS

ACKNOWLEDGMENTS

This book involved far more people than just myself. First, I would like to thank the editorial and marketing staff at New York University Press for their wise words and careful attention to detail in preparing the manuscript. Jennifer Hammer, religion editor, was particularly helpful in taking the book idea from a conversation to a full-blown project.

I am grateful for colleagues like Matthias Koenig, J. D. Payne, Margarita Mooney, Julie Park, and R. Stephen Warner, who took time out of their busy schedules to review early drafts of the manuscript, offering constructive criticism while at the same time providing encouraging words. Anonymous reviewers were also helpful in steering the book in the right direction and noticing errors in previous versions of the text. Melody Raines, my personal editor, was extremely helpful in making this book readable for a broad audience.

Many years of interacting with immigrants and hearing about their lives provided the crux of the patterns I later unearthed in quantitative data. I am extremely grateful to them for trusting me with their stories. Thanks for being friends along the journey. Thanks also to the Pew Research Center, Princeton University, Statistics Canada, and the staff at the General Social Survey and various European statistical bodies for providing their data to me and answering my questions.

Much of the data analysis in this book is based on work in earlier papers and publications. Colleagues and mentors who commented on these earlier works include Richard Alba, Delia Baldassarri, Rogers Brubaker, Mark Chaves, Alan Cooperman, Melody Crowder-Meyer, Rafaela Dancygier, Gordon De Jong, Claudia Diehl, Patricia Fernandez-Kelly, Joel Fetzer, Brian Grim, Conrad Hackett, Charles Hirschman,

Mike Hout, Elaine Howard Ecklund, Amaney Jamal, Peter Kivisto, D. Michael Lindsay, Luis Lugo, Scott Lynch, Douglas Massey, Cecilia Menjivar, Pyong Gap Min, Dan Olsen, Alejandro Portes, Darren Sherkat, Patrick Simon, Frank van Tubergen, David Voas, Robert Wuthnow, and Fenggang Yang.

Last, but by no means least, I am thankful for my supportive family, who gave me the time to write on evenings, weekends, and vacations. Thank you to my love, Kandace, and our precious ones—Ephraim, Asher, Hosanna, and Judah. You all make life worth living!

Introduction

Introducing Immigrant Faith

Four Stories of Immigrant Faith

Gurbaj Singh Multani, a twelve-year-old student at Ste-Catherine Labouré school in Montreal, Quebec, went to school on November 18, 2001, like any other seventh grader in his neighborhood. But while out on the school yard that day, his ceremonial *kirpan* (a required religious dagger for male Sikhs) fell out of its cloth sheath tucked under his clothing. Thinking nothing of it, Gurbaj picked it up and put it back into its holder. But, later in the day, news of Gurbaj's dagger, viewed by others as a weapon, reached the principal's office. Gurbaj was asked to remove the kirpan or face suspension. He chose to return home.

Gurbaj's kirpan ignited a public firestorm in Montreal, the province of Quebec, and eventually the rest of Canada. Issues of religious freedom clashed with concerns about school security. Quebecers were also trying to understand this new religious group emerging in their communities. Who are Sikhs? Where did they come from? When did they arrive? And why do they insist on bringing weapons, as Quebecers called them, to school?

Negotiations for the proper handling of the kirpan during the school day continued with the school board for months, involving Gurbaj's family, other students' parents, and school officials. But a local solution could not be found. The case eventually went to the Quebec Superior Court and later the Quebec Court of Appeal, each of which had a different view, and thus opposing decisions, on the case. Eventually, the Supreme Court of Canada found that a total ban of the kirpan violated the guarantee of religious freedom based on Canada's Charter of Rights. Five years after the initial incident, Gurbaj, then a high school senior, could legally wear his kirpan to school.

* * *

Late Easter Sunday evening in 2010, a caravan of Latino church members in three passenger vans and several cars was making its way back home to Raleigh, North Carolina, from Houston, Texas. The Buen Pastor church members of Raleigh had just finished a spiritual retreat at a church in Houston. But, as they made their way through Louisiana, the caravan was pulled over by Customs and Border Protection agents. The officers thought the group looked suspicious and pulled the caravan over in the middle of the night. Some church members had no legal status and were soon deported. Other unauthorized immigrants with children were put into deportation proceedings.

The church and sympathetic community members in North Carolina began prayer vigils and petitions and hired lawyers to defend them against this rather unusual stop by border authorities, some five hundred miles away from the U.S.–Mexico border. From their perspective, they were returning from a religious gathering, something that is fairly common for people living in the southern United States.

More than two years later, the case was administratively closed by the Department of Homeland Security (DHS) on the basis of a policy released by DHS to use discretion for cases with no public safety risk. After two years of legal wrangling, church members and community advocates were thrilled. Jorge Calderon, a church member, said, "When I heard the news that our case was administratively closed I prayed with my family in thanks to God."[1]

* * *

In the late evening of an autumn Paris night in 2005, three Muslim youths were returning home from an afternoon of soccer. Responding to reports of a robbery in the area, police picked up several young men nearby for questioning. Thinking they were also being chased by police, the three youths hid in an electrical substation where two of them, Bouna Traoré and Zyned Benna, died by electrocution. The third, Muhittin Altun, lived, but was seriously burned.

The youths' deaths sparked civil unrest in several suburbs around Paris. These communities or *banlieues* housed large numbers of Muslims, mainly from North Africa. The banlieues are known for their poverty, limited economic opportunities, and poor social conditions. Rioters burned buildings and cars, and they threw rocks at riot police night after night for several weeks. With the riots expanding throughout France, President Jacques Chirac declared a state of emergency on November 8.

Although the deaths of these two youths may have triggered the 2005 riots, it appears that tensions between police and Muslim residents living in the poverty-stricken suburbs had been running high for several months, if not years, leading up to the crisis. Cited by many media reports, one of the contributing factors to these tensions was (and continues to be) high unemployment among Muslim families throughout France. Both Muslim immigrants and their adult children complain of employment discrimination based on their Muslim-sounding names.

* * *

Like many Asian American children in the San Francisco Bay area, Jeremy Lin grew up living between the two worlds of Asian and American culture. And like his Asian peers, he was highly encouraged by his parents to pursue academics, so he became a straight-A student. But he also loved basketball, and he was good at it. In his senior year, he led his local high school team to a state title.

In 2012, "Linsanity" began. On February 4, Lin, now a Harvard-educated NBA rookie sitting on the New York Knicks' bench, was called up to play. The Knicks, after all, were playing badly, so why not give the kid a chance? Lin came off the bench with fiery determination and achieved unbelievable success. Within one week, he averaged nearly thirty points a game and gave new hope to the failing Knicks. People started asking, "Who is this kid? How did he end up in the NBA?"

As the public got to know him better, Lin made his Christian faith a central part of his public identity. Not only was he Asian, a son of immigrant parents, and obviously smart, but he was also a former leader in Harvard's Asian American Christian Fellowship and hoped to become a pastor one day. He wanted to help those in need in the United States and abroad. Under immense pressure to bring the Knicks back from the brink during the 2012 season, he said he could play without experiencing much stress because he'd "surrendered that to God. I'm not in a battle with what everybody else thinks anymore."[2]

Immigrant Faith: Here, There, and Most Everywhere

What unites these stories of Sikhs in Canada, Christians in the United States, and Muslims in France? It is *immigrant faith*. Gurbaj, a son of Indian immigrants, was living out his Sikh beliefs in a society that did not yet understand this new religious group. Church members from Buen Pastor church in Raleigh, North Carolina, were practicing a religion that was probably brought to them by missionaries from the United States but that they had replanted in the American South. North Africans in Paris moved to find a better life in Europe, only to discover that their religious affiliation limited their economic opportunities. And, Jeremy Lin, the son of Taiwanese immigrants, incorporated his inherited faith from his parents, making it a central part of his academic and athletic success.

While this book is not about daggers or deportation, banlieues or basketball, these images are inseparable from the religion of immigrants and their children. These stories of immigrant faith occurring in real time and in the real world illustrate the importance of religion within the lives of immigrants. Religion is not merely one aspect among many in immigrant lives; it can encompass everything. Immigrant faith affects daily interaction with nonimmigrants, shapes the future of immigrants in their destination society, and influences society beyond the immigrants themselves. In other words, to understand immigrants, one must understand their faith. Moreover, to understand societal change in immigrant societies, one cannot disregard the religion of immigrants.

Shelves upon shelves of books on the religion of immigrants demonstrate the recent explosion of work on the topic. Immigrant religion, which was once a rather understudied topic among both immigration and religion scholars, has become a central area of social science inquiry in anthropology, sociology, demography, and politics. Topping this off, religious practitioners and clergy are changing the focus of their work as they adapt to the growing number of immigrants in their communities. And government leaders and policy makers struggle to wrap their heads around the topic.

So why publish another book on immigrant religion? Even with the amount of scholarship on the topic, a large knowledge gap remains. Few students of religion or international migration clearly understand the role of religion in moving people across international borders, the way religion changes upon settlement in the destination country, the help or hindrance religion can be in the struggle for immigrant success, and the way immigrant religion is transmitted to further generations. This is not the case because these issues are unimportant or too confusing, but rather because up until recently, there has been a lack of the kind of quantitative data (censuses, surveys, etc.) about the religion of immigrants necessary to reveal patterns. In sum, the volume of current research on immigrant religion lacks broad-based conclusions that are applicable to most immigrants of most religions in most places.

An analogy of a tapestry may be helpful. When a tapestry is woven, each thread or section of cloth on its own tells us very little about the grander pattern displayed by a completed work. If one looks at just one section, the overall pattern may start to be visible, but it cannot be entirely confirmed. It is not until one examines the complete tapestry that patterns can be identified and single parts of it may be better understood in light of the completed project. As with a tapestry, this book's purpose is to move beyond a few cases of immigrant religion and present patterns representing entire immigrant populations for several religious groups across many immigration contexts.

Unlike most other books on immigrant religion, this text does not focus on a particular religious group. This book doesn't even spotlight a specific destination country. Instead, the book builds on previous scholarship to present big-picture patterns occurring in the religious lives of immigrants in several contexts: the United States, Canada, and Europe. This volume primarily uses quantitative data (censuses, surveys) to present a general overview of immigrant religion in the Western world. However, the real lives of immigrants are not ignored. Several vignettes help to illustrate the major points of the book, allowing the reader to make sense of statistical patterns.

This introduction to immigrant religion is not without some important assumptions and caveats. First, no central data source exists enabling researchers to consider all the various topics tied to immigrant religion in North America and Europe. Instead, this book relies on a number of data sources from several different countries to present general patterns of immigrant religious movement and adaptation. Key findings based on statistical data represent more detailed analyses performed by the author or other researchers in previous publications. Readers wanting more details on the data and methods should consult the methodological appendix.

In using data from multiple countries, this book is, unavoidably, a comparative project. For the most part, comparisons are not meant to display unique differences in destination countries of migrants. Instead, the aim of this book is to present a more common approach to the religious lives of immigrants, or patterns that remain consistent across major religious groups, irrespective of their context.

But comparisons are sometimes unavoidable, with societal differences between the American and European experiences often being the starkest. But even with this contrast, Canada, as an in-between society that has both European and American characteristics, is a helpful reference point as a middle comparison.[3] These three immigrant societies—the United

States, Canada, and Europe (more specifically Western Europe, which includes countries of the European Union in 2004 prior to enlargement, plus Norway and Switzerland)—have received nearly half of the world's immigrants. And with the exception of Australia and New Zealand, these areas are commonly known as the Western world. Consequently, this book looks at the religion of immigrants living in the West.

Second, the book does not pretend to be more than an introduction to immigrant religion. When more description and data beyond the scope of this introduction are available, the reader is pointed to resources for further reading. When more research is needed to understand the intricacies for a particular religious group, this is stated. Also, statistical data on religion usually focus on only two aspects: religious affiliation (the religious group one belongs to) and religious attendance (how frequently one attends religious services in a religious organization). Although the book mentions studies that examine the much richer religious meanings of migration and differing religious practices for a number of religious groups, it uses a rather cursory definition of religion as self-identification with a particular religious group and participation in a religious organization.[4]

Third, this book does not present the case of immigrants living outside of North America and Europe. Though immigrants living outside North America and Western Europe represent over half of the world's foreign-born population, many of these immigrant flows are more recent. Detailed research on immigrants in these places has really only begun. However, some of the key points presented in this book may still be applicable to these emerging immigrant populations around the world.

Fourth, readers familiar with the faith of immigrants will sometimes find the conclusions presented in this book's chapters to be inconsistent with their personal experience. While there are common patterns of immigrant religious adjustment, not every pattern presented in this book may be applicable to each immigrant or to all immigrant religious groups. It is important for the reader not to get caught up with how his or her experience may agree or differ from the general patterns presented here. The nature of statistical analysis is that there are always outliers. The data analysis presented in this book is based on the "average" immigrant. Further research, some of which has already been carried out, seeks to disentangle the exceptions to the rule.

Lastly, the book does not adopt a certain theoretical or ideological position. Although policy interest may be high on the topic, space is not sufficient to present policy implications.[5] Instead, this text is for the person who finds the topic of immigrant religion interesting and is searching for a quick introduction to the most basic questions surrounding the faith of immigrants and their children. To this end, extensive theoretical or policy debates are avoided, or, when necessary, are only briefly presented. These types of debates are found in a number of journals, policy briefs, and other books on immigrant religion. When applicable, the reader is pointed to these discussions throughout the text.

Moving, Changing, Integrating, and Transferring Faith

This book looks at the lives of immigrants from a life-course perspective, starting from the point of migration and the migratory journey itself, moving through the early and later days of settlement in the destination society, and ending with the religious lives of immigrant children in their adult years. As already noted, not every aspect of the lives of immigrants can be covered, but most of the highlights are examined.

Immigrants, by definition, are movers, migrating across international borders, sometimes to a country nearby or sometimes halfway around the world. As people move, so do their gods. People take their religion with them, changing both the religion they left behind in their home country and profoundly changing the religious landscape of the new country they enter. Among those who decide to take the plunge and move abroad, some may have few choices of where to move, while others may have several options available to them. All the while, religion can play an important role in their decision making, how they meaningfully understand their migration journey, and who helps them get established in the destination country.

Consequently, an immigrant faith is a *moving faith*. The first chapter answers the key question of who moves and to where, addressing the role of religion in the decisions and destinations of international migrants. Are religious people more or less likely to move internationally? Are some religious groups more likely to move than others? Do people move because of religious reasons? And if so, where do they choose to move? Does religion shape destination choice? Is an immigrant's faith used to help bring meaning to the geographic and cultural shift experienced by the immigrant? After moving, how are members of new religious groups received in the destination country? These questions help guide the first chapter's discussion.

In the case of Gubarj, the high school student in Montreal, his religious group—Sikhs—came to Canada as far back as a century ago, but moved to Canada in larger numbers during the past two or three decades. Religion played a key role for this movement as it was a defining characteristic that allowed many to be granted refugee status in Canada. As new residents, and later citizens of Canada, Sikhs continued to bring other family members from India to join them, creating a vibrant religious community first in western Canada, and over time moving eastward to cities like Montreal. Sikhs were only beginning to appear in large numbers in Quebec around the time the kirpan controversy began. Without question, for a religious minority in India, becoming an even smaller religious minority in Canada made religion an even more important part of identity for Sikhs. Understanding the religious background of migration helps us to understand why Gubarj and his family fought through several legal rounds to keep the kirpan.

Gubarj's experience in Canada also helps to illustrate how the faith of immigrants is in constant flux. Think of it. If you move to a new place, so many things change, including your faith. Cultural cues like religious holidays and accessible worship centers on every block, once present in the home country, may not line up with the new society's calendar or new neighborhood. Immigrants also have to navigate the religious scene in their new home. Not only may it take time to find their religious community, but immigrants arriving with no religion may be intrigued by all the churches around them. In fact, in some societies, religious organizations may be one of the few means to build relationships with friends from their home country or interact with the general public. Some may find themselves becoming more religious, others less so. Also, members of some religious groups may feel threatened as a religious minority in a new culture. They may seek to protect their religious heritage against the onslaught of ridicule and suspicion by the native-born population. In short, the religion of immigrants is not static. By the very nature of moving across borders and cultures, their faith is undoubtedly dynamic, hugely different from that experienced in their home country.

It could be said, then, that an immigrant faith is a *changing faith*. Chapter 2 addresses the changing contours of immigrant religion from home to new society. Are immigrants more religious after migration? Once the initial years of settlement are over, what religious patterns do immigrants adopt in their daily lives? Do immigrants switch religions from one world religion to a completely different world religion? How about immigrants with no religion: Do they become religious? Or vice versa, do some immigrants drop their religion altogether and become atheist or agnostic? If immigrants gain or lose religion, does this occur differently in different destination countries? And, what is the impact of being a minority versus a majority religion in the new society? Do minorities become more or less religious, and does this depend on how the destination country views their religious group? These questions build on each other to yield an understanding of how an immigrant's faith is constantly evolving during his or her time in the destination country.

The faith of church members at Buen Pastor church in Raleigh, North Carolina, looks rather similar to that of nonimmigrants in the southern United States. It is not uncommon to see church buses traveling along Interstate 10 going to weekend conferences or helping sister churches. After all, in comparison to other U.S. regions, the southern United States is very religious. Although the language and some religious traditions may vary slightly, these Latino immigrants' worship experience is probably quite similar to many other evangelical or charismatic worship services played out each weekend in North Carolina. It may come as a bit of a surprise that Buen Pastor is in fact a Protestant church. Most people probably think that all Central Americans are Catholic. The Buen Pastor church was probably not much different than the countless evangelical churches surrounding it. Though most of its members probably came to the United States as a transplanted church from Central America, a small number of Buen Pastor's church members could have become Protestant after migrating.

Even though they may be members of a church, a single weekend religious event may not be indicative of the daily religious regimen of some of the people on the bus. Receiving little pay for manual-labor jobs, many immigrants, especially unauthorized immigrants with few social-welfare benefits like unemployment insurance or welfare, work incredibly long hours to survive economically. This definitely impacts the time they can devote to religious services. In terms of actual worship hours, Buen Pastor's church members may even be less religious than they were in their home country.

Once having arrived in the destination society, immigrants have many choices and pressures on their lives. If they are seeking to make a permanent stay in their new country, religious groups can play an important part in helping them adjust to a new language and a new culture, navigate the job market, and prepare them to become full-fledged citizens. Religion can also help immigrants to mentally survive the emotional strain of living in a new place with such high demands on their time. But religion may not always be so positive. Being part of some religious groups, particularly if the religion is threatening to the destination country's status quo, could lead to social exclusion from employment or citizenship. Religion, then, could help, but could also hinder, immigrant success over the long term.

It is at this stage of the immigrant's life course that an immigrant faith becomes an *integrating faith.* Not only do immigrants use faith to help them integrate into society, but they also find ways to integrate their faith into their daily lives as they juggle different priorities like jobs, family, and their health. So how does immigrant religion help immigrants adjust? Are religious immigrants doing better psychologically and economically than nonreligious immigrants? Do patterns vary by religious group and destination context? For instance, how are religious minorities faring in places where new religious groups are viewed suspiciously by the general public? In such contexts, do immigrant religious minorities fare worse than the general public? And how does religion prepare immigrants to become full citizens of the destination society? These questions are addressed in chapter 3, where the influence of religion on immigrant adaptation is carefully examined.

As seen in the 2005 riots in Muslim neighborhoods in France, religion is certainly an important marker of difference for immigrants from North Africa living in France—more perhaps than for North Africans living in other countries. As many studies have shown, Muslims in Europe, many of whom are immigrants or children of immigrants, experience employment discrimination simply because they are Muslim. Consequently, religion is an important attribute that influences the integration of immigrants into society. And, with the Muslim population growing to include millions of people in Europe, the economic success of Muslims in Europe is no small matter, both for Muslims themselves and for the long-term viability of European economies. However, the same set of issues may not operate in all contexts for all religious groups. Immigrant religion in countries like the United States and Canada may help immigrants overcome difficulties rather than add to their integration problems. Whatever the case, religion can be pivotal in the economic and political adjustment of immigrants.

Finally, immigrants seek to sustain their faith traditions beyond themselves. Since most immigrants arrive as young adults, their children grow up in a culture that is different from the parents' upbringing. Often, religion becomes the vehicle by which immigrant parents transmit their values and traditions to their children, also known as the second generation. As they reach adulthood, immigrant children may face pressures from family to keep religious traditions alive. Their parents may require active involvement in religious organizations. Children may also be highly encouraged (if not forced) to marry within the religious group. And, like their immigrant parents, second-generation immigrants may use the resources available from religious communities to help them attain even higher economic success. Or, in a reverse scenario, some of the religious barriers limiting their economic opportunities that are encountered by first-generation immigrants could be passed down to their children.

In focusing on the second generation, immigrants are often *transferring faith*. Immigrant parents often seek to pass on their religion to their children. But are second-generation immigrants more or less religious than their parents' generation? And how does this tendency vary across religious groups and across different destination countries? With regard to economic prosperity, do second-generation immigrants encounter the same religious help, or perhaps hindrances, encountered by their parents' generation? Chapter 4 picks up these questions as it discusses the role of religion among second-generation immigrants.

Jeremy Lin's story illustrates many of the issues immigrant parents face in preserving their faith beyond their own generation. Jeremy may or may not be the norm, but certainly his Christian faith, encouraged at an early age by his parents, is very much part of his identity and future career ambitions. Not only does he indicate a desire to one day be involved with Christian ministries; he also uses his faith to understand his current career situation as an NBA basketball player. There could also be more to his faith story. His parents' faith, and later his own, could have been a contributing factor in his educational success. He did, after all, graduate from Harvard—no small accomplishment.

Immigrant faith is moving people all over the world, but who moves and to where? Immigrant faith is in flux following migration, but how does it change? For better or for worse, immigrant faith is important for integrating immigrants into society, but how much does it help or hinder immigrants? Immigrants seek to transfer their faith into their children, but is it really sustained? The movement of faith around the globe through migration is changing our planet. The best way to understand these global shifts is to hear from the migrants themselves, both their stories and the numbers that represent their countless stories. It is to these stories and patterns of faith that we now turn.

1

Moving Faith

Right after high school, Pedro and Lucinda were married outside Mexico City on a hot August day in 2000. The wedding was simple, but it remained a memorable celebration for the couple's family and friends. After the church ceremony, Pedro's and Lucinda's families joined together for a family portrait to commemorate this special day. But two people were noticeably missing from the photograph—Lucinda's father and brother.[1]

Lucinda's father had died several years earlier of a heart attack. Since the family's provider was no longer living, Lucinda's brother, Juan, had moved to the United States, where he could make much more money to support his mother and four younger sisters. Before Juan had left for the United States, he had worked at a local painting company. Juan and his coworker Pedro had spent many days and nights painting houses and large warehouses, and Juan had grown to trust and respect Pedro very much. So he had had no hesitation in introducing him to Lucinda. Juan had hoped the pair would date and Pedro could become, at least temporarily, *el hombre de la casa* (the man of the house). As Juan had planned, Pedro and Lucinda fell in love and began to plan their wedding. And to Juan's contentment, Pedro stuck around the house to help the family run necessary errands and be there for Lucinda's *mamá*.

While living in Lucinda's house, Pedro—a self-proclaimed agnostic—became acquainted with the Catholic Church. He didn't really enjoy going to church, but he went to mass to appease Lucinda's mother. But when their engagement was announced, Lucinda insisted on a church wedding. There was a small problem—Pedro needed to be baptized before he could be married in the church. So at the age of nineteen, Pedro joined a catechism class of twelve- to thirteen-year-olds to learn the doctrines and teachings of the Catholic Church. A few months after his baptism, Lucinda and Pedro were married.

While dating, Pedro and Lucinda discussed their dreams for their children. Lucinda heard about job opportunities from her brother and other family members in New Jersey. It sounded like a wonderful place where jobs were plentiful and life was much easier than in Mexico. Pedro and Lucinda knew that staying in Mexico City was not very promising for their future children. They also knew they could make a lot more money in the United States.

So Pedro and Lucinda, even before they were married, made the decision to go north, cross the border, and start new lives in New Jersey. As they made preparations, Lucinda grew anxious. She knew it would not be an easy journey. For support, she convinced her sister Maria to go along. With the financial help of Lucinda's brother in New Jersey, the family scrimped and saved the six thousand dollars they needed to hire a coyote (border guide) to help them cross the border. They left in October before the winter settled in.

Hiring a coyote is no guarantee of a safe passage. All three knew the risk of crossing an increasingly militarized border. What if they were to run out of food or water? What if they were robbed? Or, worse yet, what if someone tried to kidnap or shoot them? Despite the risks, the promise of a better life—and more importantly a better life for their future family—was worth it. After many hours on several buses, they arrived in Tijuana, just south of the U.S.–Mexico border. They met their coyote, who took them by car into the mountains of northern Mexico. After spending the night in a makeshift campground, they started their hike into the United States.

The journey through mountains and forests was not for the ill bodied or weak minded. The hike involved high elevations and threats from animals and other travelers, all under the cover of darkness. There was little time for sleep, food, or water. Getting across the border was actually not that hard. It was not being caught by border patrol officers and returned back to Mexico that was more challenging. Topping it all off, Maria was getting sick. She was only fifteen and just not strong enough for the journey.

The first attempt to cross the border was unsuccessful. They were apprehended in a field, charged with illegally crossing the border, and driven back to Mexico. On day two, the same scene played out. After being caught twice by border agents, they considered giving up or at least trying again later. But this would mean staying in Tijuana until they could raise enough cash to hire the coyote again. Even though Maria was exhausted, they decided to make one more try, this time going a different way.

Although they did not consider themselves very religious, if there was ever a time to pray, it was now. All three were nearing their physical and mental limits. Trust in their God was almost all they could hold onto. In those moments when they had to be motionless to avoid detection by border police, Lucinda would grab Pedro's hand and pray silently. It provided some peace before the next few steps ahead.

On the third attempt, Pedro and the coyote took turns carrying Maria on their backs. Their food and water rations were gone. It was just them, the brutal wilderness, and U.S. immigration officers. But before dawn, they managed to reach the parked van about two miles into the United States. Pedro got in, started the engine, and did not stop driving until he reached Lucinda's uncle's house in Los Angeles. After taking a few days to recover from the journey, they took a flight from Los Angeles to New Jersey to meet up with Lucinda's brother and begin their new lives.

What Is the Religion of International Movers?

Pedro, Lucinda, and Maria's journey is a true story of three people traveling the world's largest immigration corridor. Twelve million people born in Mexico now live in the United States, many of them having made a similar journey.[2] Add several million more migrants from other Central American countries who have moved to the United States, and the population of immigrants who have moved from countries south of the U.S. border numbers over twenty million people now living in the United States.

However, the migration of people across the southern U.S. border represents only about 10 percent of the world's 215 million international migrants. Although movement north into the United States is high, moving across an international border is a rare event—only about 3 percent of the world's population has done it. But if all the world's migrants were to live in a single country, it would be the world's fourth largest—smaller than Indonesia, but larger than Brazil.

Of these 215 million, about four in ten live in North America or Western Europe.[3] The United States leads the world with more than 42 million immigrants, or about one in five of all the world's migrants. Other top countries include Germany (10.8 million), Canada (7.2 million), France (6.7 million), the United Kingdom (6.5 million), and Spain (6.4 million). In these countries, immigrants constitute 10 percent or more of the total populations. Consequently, these countries in North America and Western Europe have been studied more than other immigrant destinations.

But where do these millions of migrants come from? Most migrants move from nearby countries where they can travel rather inexpensively across land or narrow sea borders. Not everyone crosses borders under darkness like Pedro and Lucinda, but many have. And illegal crossings aren't commonplace only in deserts of the southwestern United States. They are also an issue for European beach communities in Italy and Spain as well as small villages in Bulgaria and Greece. The promise of a better life in the United States or Europe is too great for migrants not to try the terrorizing and potentially deadly journey.

Other migrants move in a more formalized manner, at least from the government's perspective. For example, the United States annually accepts more than a million permanent residents.[4] About a quarter-million immigrants enter Canada each year, often after working through a point-based immigration system where language, family connections, and skills determine acceptance into the country.[5] Migrants come into Western Europe from other countries in the European Union like Poland and Romania. These migrants have the legal right to find jobs in other European countries, and many have found better jobs in the UK, Italy, or Spain. But a large number of Europe's immigrants have also come from North Africa and Turkey. These immigrants join other family members already living in Europe. Additionally, countries in Europe and North America annually accept thousands of refugees from all around the world.

In sum, most migrants to the United States and Western Europe have moved from neighboring countries or regions of the world. For example, more than half, or nearly twenty-five million, of the immigrants living in the United States have moved from the Americas, most from Mexico and other countries in Central America and the Caribbean. Most of the nearly forty million migrants who have moved into Western Europe came either from other European countries in Central or Eastern Europe or from neighboring countries in North Africa (for example, Morocco and Algeria) or nearby Turkey. Canada is an exception to this general rule as most of its immigrants have not come from nearby countries, but from Europe and Asia.

But migrants bring more than their nationality with them; they also bring their religion. Christianity comes to the United States with Latin American immigrants. Because of such high migration from south of the border, a majority of immigrants in the United States are Christian. In fact, about three in four U.S. immigrants have some Christian background, whether it is Catholic, Protestant, or some other Christian heritage. By contrast, the makeup of immigrants in Europe is not as Christian. Although immigrants from other European countries are mostly Christian, an almost equal number of non-Christian immigrants, mostly Muslim, also live in Europe. In fact, there are about as many Muslim immigrants in Western Europe as there are Christian immigrants. Canada is in the middle of this Christian/non-Christian balance

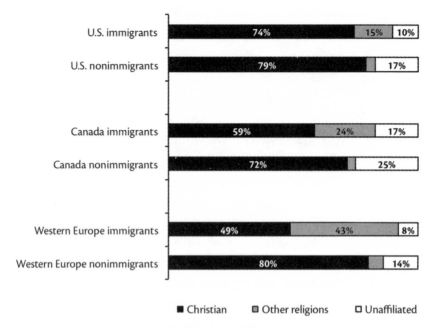

Figure 1.1. Religious distribution of immigrants and nonimmigrants in 2010. (Pew Research Center's Global Religion and Migration Database 2012; Pew Research Center's Global Religious Landscape 2012)

of immigrants. Canada has a religiously mixed immigrant population, with a slight majority of immigrants in Canada having a Christian affiliation but sizeable shares also belonging to some other religion or claiming no religious affiliation.

Percentages don't tell the whole story, however. On the world stage, the sheer volume of migration to the United States makes it the largest recipient of not only Christian but also Buddhist and religiously unaffiliated migrants. The United States likewise holds the second spot for the most Jewish immigrants (after Israel) and Hindu immigrants (after India). On the other side of the Atlantic, many European countries are also top destinations for the world's Christian migrants. But unlike the United States, European countries like Germany and France are prominent destinations for the world's Muslim migrants.

The United States, Western Europe, and Canada are all majority

Christian environments or contexts, yet they have a sizeable number of people with no religious affiliation. But broad differences in the religious breakdown of migrants in these contexts provide for a different concept of immigrants in each place. In the United States, immigrants are probably described more by their national origins than by their religion. Since the great majority is Christian or claims no religion at all—two of the most common expressions of faith within the United States—the general religious breakdown of immigrants in the United States is not that different from the percentages in the country as a whole. Partly because there is not much religious difference, Americans tend to categorize immigrants by their racial or ethnic heritage. This is especially true given America's experience with slavery and the civil rights movement—ethnic/racial distinctions have been historically more important in the United States.[6]

For example, when Pedro and Lucinda eventually made their home in New Jersey, they encountered many difficulties, but religion was not one of them. People in their small New Jersey town didn't look down on them for being Catholic. The town already had two Catholic churches and they were well-respected institutions in the community. In fact, one of the local parishes had a weekly mass in Spanish and even had a Spanish-speaking priest from Colombia. When Pedro and Lucinda did feel unwelcome, it was because they were Mexican.

In Europe, however, the religious identity and breakdown of immigrants is far more consequential. Ask the several thousand Mohammeds or Fatimas living in Western Europe how they think they are viewed by the public, and they will most likely say they are understood first as Muslims before being recognized by their nationality or ethnic group.[7] Most European countries were founded with religious differences in mind, often involving wars between Protestants and Catholics.[8] Even though many people in Europe don't attend church that much compared to those in the United States, some European countries have an official church—an entirely foreign idea to the United States, where church and state are legally separate. Add to this a Muslim immigrant population in Europe that is about equal in size to its Christian immigrant population, and immigrants become labeled more frequently by religious terms than in the United States. In fact, the most common image brought to mind when Europeans hear the word "immigrant" is a Muslim.[9]

Canada, however, with its greater assortment of immigrant religious groups and national origins of immigrants, fits somewhere between the American and European contexts.[10] Relative to the United States and Europe, Canada's share of immigrants belonging to religious minorities (non-Christian) is not as large as Europe's but also not as small as the United States'. In this way, Canada's immigrants may be viewed in more religiously and nationally diverse terms, easily adding to Canada's image as a multicultural country.[11]

All in all, the majority of immigrants in the United States are Christian, whereas about equal shares of immigrants living in Western Europe belong to Christian and non-Christian (mainly Muslim) religious groups. This demographic contrast presents different images of immigrants in each context. Whereas religious differences in the United States do not seem to be that important in describing immigrant populations, religion is an important characteristic in describing immigrants in Europe, particularly in setting apart Muslim immigrants from other immigrants.

Which Religious Groups Are More Likely to Move and to Where?

Why is the U.S. immigrant population mostly Christian, Western Europe's population split between Christian and Muslim immigrants, and Canada a bit of both? Are some religious groups more likely to move to certain places than to others? Or, are these statistics a byproduct of immigrants who would have moved anyway despite their religious background?

Many factors lead people to move across an international border. The migration decision is not a casual one but is filled with complex motives, situations, and conditions, in both the origin and the destination country. Some authors say migration involves a set of push and pull factors, often related to economic concerns.[12] This economic model is a simple example of economics 101—people living in poor economies with limited job opportunities are economically attracted to economies that are more developed and offer well-paying jobs. But immigrants consider many other factors, such as their family situation, likelihood of getting a job in the destination country, language concerns, and ability to manage once they arrive.

The total set of circumstances leading people to migrate is called "cumulative causation."[13] Although differences between national economies can lead people to move from poor to rich countries, there are many more reasons why individuals and groups move across international borders. These causes often add up to produce a migrant flow that is almost self-sustaining, lasting for several years or perhaps generations.

Economists tell us that potential migrants will include many factors on their "reasons to go" or "reasons to stay" lists. Some will include the chances of finding a job and differences in pay for the two countries, both in the short term and the long term. Others will include anticipated cultural, linguistic, and social challenges in adapting to a new place. Most potential migrants will estimate the cost of moving, including the safety risks and the up-front cash they may need to pay to enter the country. But of course, borders are not wide open. National governments may deny the entry of would-be migrants. Or unofficial means of crossing the border may be too dangerous. At the end of the day, if the would-be migrant's list of pros is greater than the cons and there is a way to enter the country, migration theorists say the would-be migrant will make the move.

But migrants do not act in a vacuum. They also have to consider their families, both immediate and extended. People may move internationally to provide for family members back home, not so much for their own personal benefit. Also, many cultures do not think in individual terms, but prioritize the family's welfare; therefore, parents, spouses, and children all weigh into the decision. In fact, some potential migrants may have little choice to migrate. Some may be expected to move when they reach a certain age, whether they like the idea or not.

Migrants will also consider their social connections or social networks in making their decision. Although pioneering migrants (the first of their family or community to move to a new country) may make their decision on the basis of individual and family factors, most migrants follow the lead of others who have already made the move. Having a brother or aunt in the destination country makes the journey and adjustment much easier. Not only can friends or family help potential migrants know how best to cross the border, but they can also help them with government red tape, and perhaps pay for their journey. Upon their arrival, family contacts can also help new immigrants find jobs and a place to live.

There are still other factors that can lead people to move across an international border. Potential migrants may come into contact with foreigners visiting their country. For example, a number of Korean and Vietnamese immigrants during the latter part of the twentieth century were spouses of military service people involved in conflicts in these countries. Also, local business people working in companies created by foreign investors may follow job opportunities presented by their colleagues in destination countries. Additionally, temporary migrants like international students, who may have only intended to stay in the destination country for a short time, may stay permanently once they become comfortable with the destination society. And, of course, we cannot forget that some migrants do not move voluntarily. Due to war or threats upon their lives, refugees will move internationally, not because they necessarily want to, but because they have to.

Because of the various factors weighing into a migration decision, certain groups are more likely to migrate than others. For example, since many migrants come from more traditional families in the developing world, men usually migrate more frequently than women. Because there is an up-front cost to moving internationally, the very poor do not usually move; instead, lower-middle-class to middle-class groups are more likely to move. Also, once a migration stream begins, it is hard to shut it off; migrants with connections in the destination country will keep coming. And it is possible that migrants are more likely to come from countries where the destination country has a historical footprint, such as former colonization, past business ventures, or previous military campaigns.

So how does religion fit into these migration models? In short, religion can influence immigrant decisions some of the time.

Let's first look at a few data points to get a sense of the role of religion in the migration of some of the largest groups around the world. Like Pedro and Lucinda, the majority of Mexicans are Catholic. From survey and census data, it appears that religion makes little difference in who has migrated from Mexico. About 85 percent of Mexicans in Mexico are Roman Catholic, and 84 percent of Mexican immigrants in the United States are also Roman Catholic, an insignificant difference. A similar story seems to exist for Turks, one of the largest immigrant groups in Germany. Turks living in Turkey are about 98 percent Muslim while foreign-born Turks living in Germany are about 95 percent Muslim. For immigrant groups originating from geographically close places and constituting an immigrant labor pool, religion is often not a direct influence on which groups go and which groups stay. It can be assumed that other factors such as those explained earlier (economic differences, family considerations, social networks) may be more pivotal in determining who moves.

However, things may not be so simple for all origin countries. Although it appears that religion is not an issue in who migrates from origin countries like Mexico or Turkey, where almost the entirety of the population belongs to a single religious group, this may not be the case for countries that are more religiously diverse or have sizeable religious minorities. Religion may influence who migrates and to where, especially if moving to the destination country involves more than crossing a land border. In these cases, the effort to migrate is higher and may take greater organization, planning, finances, and social networks.

Countries like India, Nigeria, and Vietnam are good examples of countries with emigrants who have moved all over the world, and not always to nearby countries. Although each of these origin countries has its own set of circumstances and individual situations leading people

Table 1.1. Percentage Christian in Origin Country and of Migrants from Same Origin Country in Selected Destinations

Origin country	Country's population	Migrants in U.S.	Migrants in Canada	Migrants in UK	Migrants in Austria
India	3%	9%	11%	17%	32%
Nigeria	49%	91%	85%	87%	68%
Pakistan	2%	5%	10%	3%	1%
Vietnam	8%	30%	20%	n/a	25%
Egypt	5%	62%	70%	n/a	19%

Source: Pew Research Center's Global Religion and Migration Database 2012.

to move to a new country, religion may be a factor in determining who leaves and who goes to where.

India is only 3 percent Christian, but 3 percent amounts to millions of people. According to the data we have on hand, more Christians move from India to the West than would be expected if religion were not a motivating factor. For example, more than 9 percent of Indian immigrants in the United States are Christian, while 11 percent of Indian immigrants in Canada are also Christian.[14] The percent Christian of Indian immigrants is even higher in the UK and Austria. A similar pattern exists for Nigeria, whose population is about half Christian, but whose emigrants to the same four countries are almost all Christian. In Vietnam, a small, yet identifiable, minority of the population is Christian (about 8 percent), but a greater share of emigrants from Vietnam also appears to be Christian.[15]

Similar stories of religious selection—one religious group being more likely to migrate than another—appear elsewhere in the world. In 2012, the Pew Research Center released a global study on the religious distribution of international migrants. Using a variety of census and survey data, they found a common pattern of religious minorities moving to destination countries where their religious group is the majority. Although this is not a pattern that can be tested on all migrants everywhere, the study picked up on several non-Christian examples. For instance, migrants from India (a majority Hindu country, with a sizeable Muslim minority) to Egypt (a majority Muslim country) were more likely to be Muslim.

Conversely, migrants from Bangladesh (a majority Muslim country with a sizeable Hindu minority) to Nepal (a majority Hindu country) were more likely to be Hindu than would be expected if religion were not a factor for migration.[16]

Although some religious groups may choose to migrate to certain destinations more than other groups do, this "religious" migration could still be explained by nonreligious reasons. For example, colonial ties with Britain and similar English-speaking countries may have led educated Christians, typically found in southern Nigeria or certain states of India, to find better opportunities in the West. Many refugees from Vietnam originated from South Vietnam, where the population is more Christian than in North Vietnam, leading a larger number of Christians than Buddhists or other religious groups to leave Vietnam and settle in the West.

It is important, then, to isolate the potential religious "effect" from other characteristics that lead people to migrate. For instance, could other factors like education, job skills, region of country, or wealth lie beneath what looks like a religious effect? Testing this possibility, a recent study surveyed migrants from Guatemala to the United States. While both Protestants and Catholics represent large shares of American and Guatemalan populations in the United States, the study found that emigrants were more likely to be Protestant than Catholic, regardless of age, gender, education, and personal wealth.[17] Still, there may be another factor at play. Although it cannot be determined exactly, Protestants leaving Guatemala may have been influenced by American missionaries they encountered in Guatemala. These missionaries may have provided social networks for Protestants to rely on when considering a move and eventually migrating. As before, this "religious" movement can be explained by nonreligious factors such as the presence of social networks.

While the faith of migrants can indirectly determine which groups move and to where, religion can also directly influence migration. For example, the historic Christian population in the Middle East has been decreasing in size. The decreasing share of Christians is not completely due to a sudden increase in deaths or fewer births per Christian woman but to migration. In the classic chicken-or-egg scenario, it is sometimes difficult to determine whether the Christian population is decreasing because Christians are leaving to follow friends and family who have left before them or whether religious pressures are pushing Christians out of the region. Nevertheless, religion appears to be a factor in determining which religious groups are more likely to exit the region.

It can also be assumed that religion is critically important for many of the world's international refugees. By definition, refugees are members of a persecuted group, whether because of their ethnicity, religion, or politics. Often, these three attributes of refugees are blurred so it is difficult to tease out whether a refugee movement is purely religious. Consequently, there are no official estimates of "religious" refugees. But it can be expected that they represent a large portion of the millions of international refugees. For example, most Bhutanese refugees are Hindu, pressured to leave by Bhutan's Buddhist majority. During the Iraq war, Christian refugees were far more numerous than Muslim refugees.[18]

As we have seen, the movement of groups of people across international borders can have little or much to do with religion. When the origin and destination countries are not geographically distant from each other, religion may play no role in determining which religious groups migrate. This helps to explain why the majority of migrants to the United States, mostly from Latin America, are Christian, and a large portion of migrants to Western Europe, mostly from nearby North Africa and Turkey, are Muslim. But when a longer travel distance is involved, religion can be of greater importance. Data seem to indicate that religious minorities are more likely to move, and often move to where their religious group is the majority.[19] Of course, such a general statement is not true for all migrants everywhere. It represents a pattern for only a handful of countries. As more data become available, additional research can more accurately determine whether this pattern is true around the globe.

Are Religious People More Likely to Move?

The faith of immigrants isn't only about being a Christian, a Muslim, or a member of some other religious group. It's also about personal religious experiences. These may include an immigrant's relationship with the divine, prayer life and religious beliefs, or religious service attendance. Although some immigrant religious groups are more likely to move than others, is it also possible that different types of religious people are more likely to move? In other words, are people who are more religious more likely to move?

Some migration is determined by individual-level decision making, of which religiosity (being more religious or less religious) could be a factor. It could be argued that highly religious people are too concerned with things of the spiritual realm to consider the economic benefits of migration. Or from another perspective, highly religious people may see new opportunities to share their spiritual faith if they migrate to a new country. The former example may apply to those living in monastic situations, like Buddhist monks in Thailand, while the latter example has been a common rationale for historical missionary movements, like those of Jesuit Catholics. But in both cases, these populations, at least in current history, are not large enough to reveal a general pattern across most origin and destination countries.

Nonetheless, a would-be migrant's religiosity could still matter, although its effect may not be clear-cut. For example, early U.S. history is replete with examples of highly religious Puritans and Calvinists (Protestant sects or minorities in Europe at the time) making their way to America in search of religious freedom and the establishment of a new religious utopia. From this historical evidence, it would appear that more highly religious people are more likely to migrate. But we also know from U.S. history that people moved to the United States and within the United States in search of economic gain, examples being the establishment of plantations in the U.S. South or the gold rush in the U.S. West. It does not appear that these migrants were that religious; instead, they were searching for a quick dollar in the hopes of making it rich.[20]

Move ahead to current times and the picture is no less clear. Although there is little data demonstrating whether religious people are more likely to migrate, there are a few data points that help us understand whether personal religiosity influences someone to cross an international border. For instance, the New Immigrant Survey in the United States surveyed new permanent residents of the United States in 2003.[21] About half of these respondents were new arrivals coming directly from another country. Interviews took place about four to six months after migration and included several questions about religion. One question asked about religious service attendance in the last country of residence prior to moving.[22] If it is assumed that the new immigrants accurately remembered their religious attendance levels before migration, their answers to this question can be compared with the estimated percentage of the origin country's population who attend religious services monthly or more frequently.[23]

For most origin countries of recent migrants to the United States, the survey revealed no clear picture of how religiosity or, in this case, religious service attendance, has a bearing on international migration. The share of new immigrants from China, Nigeria, and Poland regularly attending religious services is about the same as the share of people attending services in the general population in their origin countries. However, more new immigrants from the Dominican Republic, India, the Philippines, and Vietnam seem to attend religious services than in the general population in their countries of origin. By contrast, new immigrants from Mexico were less likely to attend religious services monthly or more frequently than their peers in Mexico.[24]

A different study of internal migrants within the United States does find that religious activity may have a small impact on migration.[25] The study shows that migrants with a high involvement in church social activities are less likely to move than those with little or no social involvement in a religious organization. The author of the study theorizes that

Table 1.2. Percentage Attending Religious Services Monthly or More

Origin country	Origin country population (1999–2001)	New immigrants in U.S. (2003)
China	3%	5%
Dominican Republic	54%	**77%**
India	51%	**75%**
Mexico	74%	**64%**
Nigeria	95%	90%
Philippines	79%	**90%**
Poland	78%	78%
Vietnam	13%	**38%**

Sources: Origin: World Values Survey Round 4. Immigrant: New Immigrant Survey.

Note: Bold type indicates significant differences of immigrants from origin country within a 95 percent confidence interval. Survey weights applied to all estimates.

it takes considerable time and energy to build up a social network of religiously minded people, and moving could involve too much effort to rebuild these relationships. Although this article demonstrates that more social activities lead to lower migration, the study's findings are more sociological than theological. This same situation could exist for people who are involved with any civic group, religious or nonreligious, in their community.

Pedro and Lucinda's story is purely anecdotal and not representative of all migrants from Mexico to the United States, but it is striking how it mirrors the apparent lack of importance religion may play on individual-level decisions leading to migration. Although Lucinda and Pedro are Roman Catholic, their decision to migrate was not based on personal religious commitment, but mostly on family and economic considerations. According to data from Mexico, there is no indication that Pedro and Lucinda were unusually more or less religious than the average Mexican living in Mexico. They didn't go to mass every week, but like the majority of Mexicans, they made it to church about once a month.

However, the apparent disconnect between religious activity and the likelihood to migrate does not imply that faith is unimportant to migrants or rarely used in their journey. After all, Pedro and Lucinda's crossing of the U.S.–Mexico border was a perilous trip. In such dangerous moves, leaning on spiritual support is not unusual. Not surprisingly, and probably like many others before them, Pedro and Lucinda put their trust in their God during the most trying moments of the journey.

Pedro and Lucinda's example is not unique, particularly among those crossing into the United States from Latin America. Jacqueline Hagan, in her book *Migration Miracle,* writes about the role of faith in migratory movements from Central America to the United States. She interviewed several religious leaders, migrant families, and recent migrants to understand the spiritual nature of these migrations and how faith is used at each step of the journey. According to Hagan, religion is used from the point of decision to move to the process of preparing for and making the trip and, finally, during resettlement in the United States.

The sentiments of faith, hope, and meaning are also present in the stories of immigrants from Europe during the wave of migration to the United States in the late nineteenth and early twentieth centuries. Pulitzer Prize–winning author Oscar Handlin describes Italian migration as "the whole drama of salvation."[26] Just as Christ migrated from heaven to earth experiencing great pain and eventually death, the experience of Italian immigrants in the United States was also hard. But, in Christ's conquering of death through his resurrection, immigrants have found the hope to carry on. They believed that tomorrow—if not the future lives of their children—would be better.

From European immigrants more than a century ago to Latino immigrants today, it is not unusual for labor migrants in the United States to describe their migration in spiritual terms. It is common for many to use religious imagery, symbols, and narratives to understand the trials and challenges of their migration, not to mention their transition to American life. But this does not necessarily mean that migrants coming from these countries represent the most religious people of their communities. Almost anyone who goes through these arduous journeys would call out to a divine being in his or her time of need. Hagan writes,

Religion does not explain why the individual people decided to migrate, nor does it directly determine whether they successfully made it to the United States. Yet, as a powerful guiding, coping, protective, and mediating force, religion did shape how these migrants formed their decisions, how they decided on the timing of their departures, how they experienced the journey, and ultimately how they made sense of their place in the migration process.[27]

These two aspects of religion and migration—average religiosity prior to moving, yet significant religious experiences while moving—can co-exist. The more and less religious are equally likely to migrate; however, migrants experiencing harrowing moves, whether physically difficult journeys or incredibly trying bureaucratic hurdles, may still paint their migration experience using religious strokes.

While migrants may be equally religious or nonreligious before moving, for some origin countries, other factors leading some people to migrate more frequently than others may be indirectly tied to religion. For example, in many parts of the developing world, the less educated are found in small towns and more rural areas. Perhaps because of their harsh environments or low levels of education, religion may be more important to those living in rural areas than to those living in more urban areas.[28] Labor migration from bordering countries often appeals more to people from rural or semirural areas, and may potentially, yet indirectly, draw religious people. This could be a contributing explanation for the apparently high religiosity of Muslim immigrants in Europe. Many of the first immigrants from Turkey were from villages and rural areas of central Turkey. A similar outflow of migrants from North Africa to France, Belgium, and the Netherlands also occurred. And because of social networks, these migration chains through family networks continue today, potentially leading to a more religious flow of migrants. As another example, most migrants from India moving to the West represent higher classes where active religious involvement is more highly expected than in lower classes. In this way, migrants are selected on the other end of the class spectrum, but the same result occurs—more religious citizens end up moving.

In short, there is no concise answer to the question whether more religious people migrate. If more religious people are more likely to migrate, this tendency probably occurs more indirectly, either by class or region within the source country. However, the general pattern is that personal religiosity does not play a crucial role in leading people to migrate. Still, this apparent lack of influence of religiosity on migration can be held in tandem with the phenomenon of migration as a "theologizing experience."[29] Some migrations are particularly difficult, and understanding the challenges through a spiritual lens can bring meaning and comfort to an immigrant's troubles.

If migrants are, on average, not any more religious than those who stay behind, why do immigrants appear to be a fairly religious group of people? Although it may be true that immigrants are more religious than nonimmigrants in some destination countries, this does not mean that the immigrants were more religious than nonmigrants in their country to begin with. The origin country could simply be more religious than the destination country. Also, immigrants can change their religious activity after migrating. For a variety of reasons (to be explored in chapter 2, "Changing Faith"), the religious patterns of migrants rarely stay the same. In sum, although immigrants may be a religious group of people, this does not imply that religious people are more likely to migrate. There are many other processes that could be happening in both origin and destination countries.

How Are Immigrant Religious Groups Welcomed after Moving?

Migrants arriving in a new country are not entering places void of history or social conventions. As migrants become immigrants (residents of the destination society), the degree of welcome they receive can severely affect their future in the new country. Even though some societies may have long histories of migration and years of experience with immigrants, the general public may not eagerly welcome all immigrants. Countries with shorter histories of migration may be even less welcoming since they have less experience interacting with foreigners and different cultures. And the environment immigrants settle in is more than only historical. Each destination society also has a certain way of doing business, ordering political life, and practicing religion.

These differences in destination societies, also called contexts of reception, can have a profound impact on an immigrant's future. Immigration scholars Alejandro Portes and Rubén Rumbaut place different contexts of reception along a continuum.[30] On one end of the spectrum, some societies exclude immigrants, permitting them to exist within society but, for all intents and purposes, segregating them from active participation within society. On the other end of the spectrum, societies actively encourage immigrants to be part of society, offering them financial and social assistance to help them adjust to their new surroundings. In the center stand societies that passively accept immigrants. These societies tolerate immigrants but offer little assistance to them. Their economic and social success is dependent on their own hard work, ingenuity, and social connections.

As already mentioned, demographics can shape the way immigrants are viewed within society. Even the number and composition of immigrants can alter people's views of immigrants, including their immigrant religions. For example, there are about twelve million Muslim immigrants living in Europe—about the same as the number of Mexican immigrants living in the United States.[31] The large number of Muslim immigrants in Europe has an impact on immigration debates and whether immigrants are viewed primarily as a religious or an ethnic group. The boundary line marking differences between immigrant and nonimmigrant groups seems to be religious in Europe. But while the discussion in Europe is focused on Muslims as the most important group, media reports in the United States focus on Mexican immigrants or Latinos as the largest immigrant group. This is not a religious distinction, but an ethnic marker. Despite various backgrounds, origin countries, and languages that make up Latinos in the United States and Muslims in Europe, both are viewed as "immigrant" groups, and consequently not yet a full part of American or European societies.[32]

Not only can immigrant group size shape the way immigrants are described, whether by religious or by ethnic terms, but the prevalence of immigrants within religious groups can also influence the way those religions are viewed by the general public. For instance, in many immigrant societies, religious minorities are largely made up of immigrants. In the past, U.S. immigrant religious groups used to be Catholics and Jews, and the general population was resistant to welcoming them because they seemed overwhelmingly foreign. But over time, Catholics and Jews have become an integral part of mainstream American society.[33] Currently,

Table 1.3. Religious Groups by Total and Immigrant Populations

Religion	Total population	Immigrant population	% Immigrant
United States			
Christian	243,100,000	32,000,000	13%
Muslim	2,770,000	2,100,000	76%
Unaffiliated	50,980,000	4,400,000	9%
Buddhist	3,570,000	1,700,000	48%
Hindu	1,790,000	1,300,000	73%
Jewish	5,690,000	370,000	7%
Other religion	2,530,000	940,000	37%
Canada			
Christian	23,470,000	4,200,000	18%
Muslim	710,000	670,000	94%
Unaffiliated	8,050,000	1,300,000	16%
Buddhist	290,000	290,000	>99%
Hindu	470,000	310,000	66%
Jewish	350,000	140,000	40%
Other religion	690,000	320,000	46%
Western Europe			
Christian	298,470,000	25,870,000	9%
Muslim	19,490,000	12,660,000	65%
Unaffiliated	85,680,000	4,440,000	5%
Buddhist	1,150,000	960,000	83%
Hindu	1,270,000	810,000	64%
Jewish	1,100,000	190,000	18%
Other religion	1,590,000	1,460,000	92%

Sources: Pew Research Center's Global Religion and Migration Database 2012; Pew Research Center's Global Religious Landscape 2012.

Table 1.4. Percentage Not Wanting Neighbors Who Are Immigrants or of a Different Religion

Country	Immigrants or foreign workers	Of a different religion
United States	13%	3%
Canada	5%	2%
Finland	17%	10%
France	43%	30%
Great Britain	16%	2%
Germany	16%	5%
Netherlands	10%	3%
Norway	8%	3%
Spain	8%	7%
Sweden	2%	2%
Switzerland	8%	5%

Source: World Values Survey Round 5 (2006).

Note: Survey weights applied to all estimates.

with the exception of Jews, most non-Christian religious groups in the United States, Canada, and Western Europe are comprised mostly of immigrants. Today, religions like Islam, Hinduism, and Buddhism are often regarded as "immigrant" faiths. By being labeled as adherents of one of these foreign religions rather than of a more integrated religion, immigrants who practice minority faiths can, in some societies, feel less welcomed than if they were part of the majority religious group.

To get a sense of how immigrants are welcomed by members of Western societies, surveys ask about a number of attitudes toward immigrants. One question often used as an indicator of the general public's welcome toward immigrants is who people would or wouldn't like as neighbors. For instance, more than one in ten people in the United States would prefer not to have immigrants or foreign workers as neighbors. By contrast, the percentage of people in several European countries who would not like to have an immigrant neighbor is higher. For example, in Finland, Great Britain, and Germany, nearly two in ten people don't want an immigrant neighbor, while the ratio is about four in ten for those living in France. Canadians are the most willing to have immigrants as neighbors as fewer than one in ten would not want an immigrant neighbor.

There is a similar pattern of less welcoming attitudes in Europe when people are asked whether they would want a neighbor belonging to a different religion. Only a small percentage of people in the United States (3 percent) prefers not to have a neighbor belonging to a different religion. However, in Europe, several countries have much higher rates of people not wanting a person of a different religion near them, including those living in Finland (10 percent) and France (30 percent). Only a small percentage of Canadians (2 percent) would not want someone of a different religion living near them.

At a governmental level, policies toward immigrants and religious groups can also dramatically vary across countries. The Migration Integration Policy Index (MIPEX) measures whether policies toward immigrants are more favorable or less favorable. Somewhat following the pattern found in the survey data, policies toward immigrants are less favorable in most Western European countries and more favorable in the United States and Canada.[34]

In terms of religion, some countries provide legal protections for majority religious groups. For instance, several European countries have a legally established state church, to which they extend educational, welfare, or tax benefits. By contrast, there is less governmental favoritism for official religious groups in North America, where the church and state are legally separate. Quantifying these differences, religious favoritism indices provided by the Pew Research Center place most Western European countries on the higher end of the index, often ranging from an index score of 0.3 to 1.0 on a 0-to-1 scale. By contrast, the United States has a quite low religious favoritism score, falling below 0.1. Canada sits in between most European countries and the United States, with a score of 0.55.[35]

Higher religious favoritism for majority religious groups in Europe does not imply that Europeans are more religious than Americans. Far from it: many studies point to higher religious activity in the United States than in Western Europe. For example, about four in ten Americans attend religious services monthly or more frequently, while the number is

only two in ten for Western Europeans. As has been typical for the U.S.–
Europe comparison, Canada sits again in the center, with about three
in ten Canadians attending religious services monthly or more often.[36]

Why do these contextual differences matter for immigrant faith? The
welcome of immigrants, whether experienced within their demographic
situation or through governmental regulations, can dramatically alter an
immigrant's faith. For example, Pedro and Lucinda were never ridiculed
for being Catholic. In fact, in attending their local Catholic parish, they
were able to stay connected to the larger Mexican community. Additionally, they were able to receive food and clothing from a number of
Protestant churches in their area that were helping immigrants. But the
experiences of a Mohammed or a Fatima in Europe could be much different. They may not only find it difficult to get a job because they are
Muslim, but they would also be considered non-European in clinging to
their traditional religious practices.

Taking demography, people's attitudes, governmental policies, and
religious backdrops all into consideration, two contrasting contexts of
reception for immigrant religious groups emerge in the United States
and Western Europe. In the United States, the majority of immigrants are
Christian and enter a society that is fairly religious. By contrast, almost
equal shares of immigrants in Western Europe are Christian and Muslim, but both religious groups are entering a context that is relatively
less religious than the United States. Europe has harsher policies toward
immigrants than the United States and also has higher anti-immigrant
and anti–religious-minority attitudes. Europe's governments are also
more likely to favor religious-majority groups than the United States.
Meanwhile, Canada, with a somewhat religious population, a mixed
Christian/non-Christian immigrant population, and some government
favoritism toward religious groups, has attributes of both American and
European contexts.

These differing contexts of reception, as will be explained in later chapters, create very different atmospheres for immigrant religious groups. In
broad terms, religion has been described as a bridge for immigrants in

their adjustment to American society, but a barrier in Europe.[37] Because religious minorities represent a smaller share of the population in the United States than in the European context and because America is more religious than Europe, immigrants are more welcomed, and sometimes encouraged, to use their religion in helping them adapt to American society. By contrast, religion is more frowned upon by the European public, especially when the minority religious group is as large a population as is currently found among Muslim immigrants in Europe. Consequently, religion, both in terms of religious identity and religious practice, could hinder Muslim immigrant adjustment in Europe.

A Moved Faith or a Faith Move?

Pedro and Lucinda's story of moving from Mexico to the United States is not necessarily representative of all Mexican immigrants in the United States, but their story does seem to agree with census and survey data. Religion did not drive them to make a decision to migrate. And as part of the Roman Catholic majority in Mexico, they were not any more or less likely than other religious groups to leave Mexico and travel to the United States. Also, they seemed about as religious as the average Mexican. In these respects, Pedro and Lucinda's faith was not what moved them but rather a faith that moved with them as a simple consequence of their migration.

But this does not mean that Pedro and Lucinda completely disregarded their faith in the process. It played an important part in their understanding of their journey. It also helped them mentally survive the perilous journey across the border. In these ways, Pedro and Lucinda's faith was moving for them, not in a migratory sense, but as an emotional and spiritual comfort.

Looking past religious affiliation to religious activity, researchers have not found that more religious migrants are more likely to move. Studies demonstrate either a mixed picture of more and less religious people migrating internationally or no differences in migration by religious activity. Therefore, the idea that immigrants are highly religious is best explained by other processes, perhaps a move from a location with high religiosity within the origin country itself or a change in religious activity after migration. Nonetheless, this does not mean that immigrants won't use their faith to help them during the journey or to bring meaning to their difficulties. As immigrants like Pedro and Lucinda move to new countries, their religion is a moved faith. Religion doesn't necessarily lead them to move. Instead, their faith moves along with them, sometimes helping them with the journey.

Pedro and Lucinda's story may be different from that of others migrating *from* or *to* other countries, or even from those of other immigrants in the United States. Some religious groups, like Muslims, are more highly represented among immigrants in Europe, while immigrants in the United States are majority Christian. It appears, however, that for most origin countries of migrants, especially those far from the destination countries, minority religious groups are more likely to move than majority religious groups. The fact that greater number of Christians migrate to the United States, Canada, and several Western European countries from countries where Christianity is not the majority religion serves as one of many examples of this pattern found around the world. Although historical and social explanations may underlie the religious selection of migrants, it is a rather common occurrence that cannot be ignored. In this way, religion can be a factor in determining who moves and to where, leading to a faith move.

Lastly, migrant religious groups are greeted differently across countries. In particular, contexts of reception in the United States and Europe differ substantially. In the United States, with lower governmental regulations of religion, a relatively religious society, rather positive attitudes toward immigrants, and an immigrant population that religiously looks like the mainstream population, immigrants may use religion in their adjustment to American society and in forming their identity as new Americans. By contrast, Europe's legal favoritism of majority religious groups, its rather religiously inactive population, its less welcoming social context for immigrants and religious minorities, and its large immigrant Muslim population may make religion more of a hindrance for immigrant adjustment, particularly for Muslim immigrants. Canada's context of reception for immigrant religious groups sits somewhere between those of the United States and Europe, containing features of both contexts; therefore, it is possible that religion may be a help for some immigrants in Canada but a hindrance for others. It is these latter issues of incorporating immigrants into Western societies and the role of religion therein that are the focuses of the next two chapters. First up, how an immigrant faith changes after migration.

2

Changing Faith

Guo Kai Li, her husband, Zhang Yi, and their daughter, Emily, moved to Montreal, Canada, in the summer of 2001. Like so many other mainland Chinese emigrating to Canada at the time, they were excited to start new lives in a new place. After several years of waiting for their immigration visas, the delay was finally over. They had arrived in a world-class city where they could make a fresh start in their careers, raise their young daughter, and one day become citizens of Canada.

As soon as they got off the plane, they joined the immigration queue. Despite the long journey, they were so excited to finally be in Canada. After stamping their passports, the border patrol officer motioned to the side, pointing them to the large exit doors. The officer said, "Welcome to Canada and Bienvenue à Québec." Guo Kai Li and Zhang Yi looked at each other with confusion. They knew they were in Canada, and they had planned on settling in Quebec, but why the sudden change to French? Wasn't Montreal an English-speaking city?

Almost everything about Montreal was as they expected: a large metropolitan city, tall buildings, people going here and there. But a few things did not meet their expectations. One was the language. Every street sign was in French. The hotel employees greeted them in French and spoke only a few words of English. Then there was the lease contract for their first apartment—again, only in French. As days went on, they began to wonder if they had made a mistake. This city was far more French-speaking than all the websites had indicated. Maybe they had chosen the wrong city. How would they find a job when they couldn't speak a lick of French? They had practiced English for years, preparing for this moment, and now it seemed as though all those English classes were worthless.

Also, they were impressed by the number of churches. Whenever they went for a walk around the city, they saw church after church after church. They had heard about a church somewhere in Beijing, but they had never visited it. Like most mainland Chinese, Guo Kai Li and Zhang Yi didn't believe in any god. That type of thinking was for their ancestors. They relied on themselves and science to succeed, not an imaginary, fictitious being. Nevertheless, on a warm summer day, they decided to visit L'Oratoire Saint Joseph, the world's largest shrine to Saint Joseph. It is a popular tourist destination in Montreal, and all the tourist books said it was a must-see. Although the images of Mary, Joseph, and Jesus were confusing to them, they marveled at the artistry, especially the grand stained-glass windows. Although a church building could be found on almost every block, Guo Kai Li and Zhang Yi rarely saw people go in or out of any of them. Like most Quebecers have done for years, Guo Kai Li and Zhang Yi started to mentally block out all the churches they passed by.

Within a few months, Guo Kai Li and Zhang Yi began to find their way around Montreal, making their best attempt to make a go of it. After all, it was the most affordable urban center in Canada—an important factor in trying to adjust to a new country. Zhang Yi decided not to look for a job right away. He had heard that most Canadian companies would not accept his Chinese education, so he decided to go back to school and get a degree in finance. It would be a four-year degree, but the Quebec government provided a grant for families of students. They could live on this grant and perhaps use some of their savings. Meanwhile, Guo Kai Li heard of government-sponsored French classes offered at a local community center. The government gave language students a stipend and offered free child care. She could learn French, have time off from caring for her daughter, and earn extra spending money—what a deal! She also heard that about half the class consisted of Chinese immigrants, so it would help her meet some people from her country.

By fall, Guo Kai Li, Zhang Yi, and their daughter, Emily, were all in their classes. They found the transition back to school challenging but were excited to have these opportunities. But as the winter winds started coming a few months later, Guo Kai Li and Zhang Yi hit a wall. Guo Kai Li's mother's health was failing in China, and she longed to be closer to her. Emily was not enjoying her French-only daycare. Guo Kai Li was doing alright in her French classes, but was frustrated at how long it was taking to say only a few simple phrases. And Zhang Yi was finding it difficult to be a student again. He had never taken university courses in English before and he was fifteen years older than everyone else in his program.

Despite the difficulties, Zhang Yi mustered enough perseverance to soldier on. But Guo Kai Li's mind kept wandering back to their visit of Saint Joseph's Oratory. The wall paintings showed Jesus helping many people in need. She also remembered how her grandmother in China would read Bible stories to her as a child. She began to doubt whether her Chinese parents and teachers were right—was God really a hoax? Because if there was a god, any god, perhaps he could help her family during this difficult time.

During Guo Kai Li's lunch break, one of her classmates, Gao Su, talked about a gathering he had had at his house the weekend before. He told Guo Kai Li that it was actually a church. Not a church like those Guo Kai Li had seen scattered throughout Montreal, but a group of people who met together to pray and study the Bible. After a bit more conversation, Gao Su could see she was interested in the idea and invited her to their next meeting. Guo Kai Li was excited to go. At the very least, it would be a fun evening to spend with friends from China, something she had missed during the past few months.

But Guo Kai Li didn't attend only the first church meeting. She became a regular. She grew more and more curious about these *Jīdū tú* (Christians), as they called themselves. She started reading the Bible regularly and even found herself praying from time to time. Over the next year, she found that the church meetings gave her a peace she had not sensed before, especially given the turmoil of adjusting to a new place. Over time, Guo Kai Li became convinced that God did exist, and she was baptized by the church's pastor the following summer.

However, Zhang Yi had a different spiritual experience than his wife. He was too busy studying for exams to take four hours off each Saturday evening to study the Bible. But he knew it was helping his wife, so he didn't keep her from going to the church group. Zhang Yi would sometimes join the group during special events like Chinese New Year or Christmas. He enjoyed the friendship. But the God stuff was too much for him, strange and, in his opinion, unnecessary. In the end, Zhang Yi did not reach the level of commitment to the church group shown by his wife. For Zhang Yi, his faith was pretty much the same as it was in China, rather nonexistent. For Guo Kai Li, however, her faith had changed dramatically.

How Does Moving Change an Immigrant's Faith?

Moving internationally can be a pivotal, life-changing event, and often a spiritual one. However, even though migrants may use religious words to describe their migration, this doesn't always mean they are more religious after moving. In other words, migration can be a spiritual event, but this does not necessarily result in a religious revival among immigrants. In fact, quite the opposite situation seems to occur.

Migrants face a daunting adjustment to their new country after moving. In trying to find a job, immigrants face many uncertain, stress-filled days. Depending on the local economy, finding a good job, or any job, can take time. Then immigrants need to figure out how they can advance in their jobs. Do they need to learn more English? Should they go back to school? Should they look at alternative job opportunities? All the while, immigrants are making their way in the new country, charting the best path forward.

Beyond economic insecurity, immigrants also live in a foreign country with foreign rules of social engagement, a foreign language, and a foreign culture. However much immigrants prepare before moving, there will still be surprises. Even people who move to a new city, let alone cross an international border, have to find new doctors, change addresses, find the best places to shop, and find new schools for their children. All this takes even more time and energy for international immigrants.

In the midst of all these changes and this mental chaos, immigrants also have their spiritual lives to consider. Although migration as a major life event may cause some to be more open to spiritual things, this does not mean they immediately become religiously active in a local faith community. In fact, it is possible that immigrants, at least in the short term, may go to churches, mosques, or other religious gatherings less frequently than in their home country.[1] Often, the pressure of adapting puts religious activity at the bottom of the list. It can take time before immigrants pick up their religious patterns where they left off in their home country. And it is possible that they will never be as religious as they were before.

Guo Kai Li and Zhang Yi experienced these types of adjustments first-hand. Although neither was religious before migrating, finding a religious group, despite all the churches they saw in Montreal, was not a high priority, at least at first. They were first trying to navigate their way through apartment leases, select the best education programs, and keep their daughter happy. Involvement in a religious organization was far from their minds. Surviving and setting up their future lives was far more important.

Survey data show how immigrant religious attendance drops after migration. In 2003, immigrants receiving their permanent residency (green cards) in the United States were asked about their current and previous religious attendance in their home country before coming to the United States. About half of the survey respondents were interviewed four to six months after arriving in the United States. The other half had lived in the United States for a year or longer, and were adjusting their temporary status to permanent.

For every major religious group, immigrants indicated that they attended religious services less frequently in the United States than in their home country.[2] This was true for both groups—new arrivals and those adjusting their immigration status. Although this drop in religious participation was greatest for new arrivals (remember, they had only been in the United States for a few months), a lower share of those adjusting their status also attended religious services compared with those in their home country. For example, 84 percent of Catholic new arrivals attended religious services monthly or more before moving, but 52 percent did so after migration. The drop among Catholic adjustees is smaller—79 percent to 50 percent—but still a significant decline. And the pattern of decline is consistent across all religious groups. Other Christian immigrants such as Christian Orthodox and Protestants also experience a 20 percent or more drop among new arrivals and a 10 percent–plus drop for adjustees.[3] Non-Christian groups also experience a disruption in their religious attendance patterns. Muslim, Buddhist, and Hindu immigrants are all less likely to attend religious services in their new lives compared with their premigration lives.

Although this pattern of decline is quite consistent, this decrease in religious attendance from pre- to postmigration is contrary to many studies conducted during the 1990s.[4] Researchers found that migrants were swarming to religious centers to seek help in their adjustment to the United States.[5] In these studies, immigrants spoke of harrowing journeys of faith and how they were more religious in America than in their home country. But these studies were not revealing the whole picture. Researchers were able to interview only those immigrants already worshipping in religious organizations. In other words, no one heard the stories of Christian immigrants working part-time jobs on Sunday mornings or Muslim immigrants having to miss Friday prayers because their boss wouldn't give them the time off.

Also, it appears that this drop in immigrant religious attendance is not only an American phenomenon. Studies of new immigrants in the

Table 2.1. Percentage Attending Religious Services Monthly or More by Migration and Religion

Religious group and migration timing	Premigration	Postmigration
Catholic new arrivals	84%	**52%**
Catholic adjustees	79%	**50%**
Christian Orthodox new arrivals	71%	**41%**
Christian Orthodox adjustees	61%	**52%**
Protestant new arrivals	80%	**55%**
Protestant adjustees	74%	**60%**
Muslim new arrivals	46%	**20%**
Muslim adjustees	48%	**21%**
Buddhist new arrivals	27%	**13%**
Buddhist adjustees	38%	28%
Hindu new arrivals	77%	**36%**
Hindu adjustees	61%	**43%**
Other religion new arrivals	76%	**42%**
Other religion adjustees	58%	50%

Source: New Immigrant Survey 2003.

Note: Bold type indicates significant differences between pre- and postmigration within a 95 percent confidence interval.

province of Quebec arriving in the 1990s as well as recent arrivals in Germany and the Netherlands before 2010 report a similar drop in religious attendance following migration.[6] As in the United States, this drop occurs for both Christian and non-Christian groups.

Nevertheless, the decline in religious attendance after migration should not be surprising.[7] Many other things in an immigrant's life are also disrupted after moving. Not only are relationships with family and friends changing, but immigrants can experience short-term joblessness. And decisions like having a baby might be put off for several months or years until immigrants are more certain about their future.[8] Some immigrants do not intend to stay in the destination country beyond a year or two. If they are temporary, they have less incentive to get involved in local groups, religious or nonreligious.

Religious reasons can also explain this drop in religious attendance. Many immigrants move from a country where their religious group is the majority. But when arriving in the new country, they may find themselves members of a religious minority or may find that they are in a smaller majority group. Also, most immigrants move from a country where there is one, maybe two, dominant religious groups. But many Western societies, including those in Europe, contain many religious groups to choose from. These religious contextual changes can dampen religious attendance. Although the exact process is unknown, the variety of religious choices and the corresponding lack of people belonging to the same faith create a situation where immigrants can become perplexed, not knowing which religious group is theirs or not wanting to make the effort to figure it out.[9]

This type of religious perplexity is not an insult to an immigrant's intellect. Guo Kai Li, for example, is highly educated. But her religious background was sparse and her familiarity with faith in general, and more specifically with Christianity, was limited. Even though she eventually joined a church, she didn't do so until several months after migrating, and even then, she was not quite sure if the group she joined was legitimate. Coming from an atheist country, she eventually came to terms with living in a society where faith was present; but it took her a while to navigate the options, understand them, and figure out whether faith was important for her future. A similar process can occur for Protestants from Latin America trying to decipher whether the religious group they are joining is similar to the one they belonged to back home. Also, there are many different strands of Muslim, Hindu, and Buddhist religious groups, with immigrant religious groups not looking exactly the same as in their home country.

For immigrants, moving to a new country involves many changes—a new economy, new relationships, but also a new religious scene. It can take time to understand each sphere of life, and often religion is a lower priority. Because of these reasons, immigrants are generally less religious after moving between countries. But this does not mean this disruptive change is permanent. Once immigrants become adjusted, religious patterns can resume, but perhaps not the same patterns as before.

Do Immigrants Change Their Religious Practices?

Although Guo Kai Li was not religious in her home country, faith became important for her after she moved to Canada. There was a change, mostly driven by a change in countries. For if she had not moved to Montreal, had not seen the many churches, and had not come into contact with other Chinese of faith, her faith (or lack thereof) in China might have stayed about the same. Even though Guo Kai Li didn't have a faith that moved with her, her faith changed once she settled into Canadian life.

Many things change after an immigrant moves around the world or even across a border only a hundred miles away. Immigrants start speaking the new country's language much more. They start eating different foods. They may even wear different clothes. Some adaptations are intentional. For instance, immigrants may get a better education to improve their chances in competing for jobs with nonmigrants. Other changes can be less intentional. Immigrants may adopt new ways of saying things or celebrate new holidays, all in the process of adapting to the new culture around them.

In recent years, migration scholars have debated whether immigrants keep their cultural ways and values in our ever-globalizing and multicultural world, or whether they adapt to the new country's ways, even when the pressure to do so may not be as great as in decades past.[10] The debates come to different conclusions, but several experts agree that at a minimum, immigrants are adjusting somewhat to the new country, even though they may not feel forced to do so. In fact, it was suggested by scholars long ago that the adaptation process is rather natural and can occur unintentionally at times.[11]

Religious adaptation can happen in a number of ways. For example, immigrant religious groups, regardless of their faith traditions, may resemble over time the form and style of Protestant congregations.[12] For example, even though Hindus in India may not go to a temple every week or have religious instruction classes for children, many Hindus in the

United States do regularly attend a Hindu worship center and have Hindu Sunday schools. In this way, Hindu immigrants in the United States are adapting their religious organizations to the congregational form that is so prevalent in the United States.[13]

As another example, national networks of Muslims have developed in Western Europe and the United States, sometimes for political advocacy or institutional support. These organizations follow a structure similar to those of Christian denominations in these countries, often seeking to influence public policy or support the growth of the religious group beyond its current membership.[14] These types of networks are less present in the countries Muslim immigrants have come from, so their development appears to be a religious adaptation to the form of religion commonly practiced in the West.

Also, religious traditions can change, becoming more like those in the new country. For example, Muslim women in the United States are much more likely to attend Friday prayers at a mosque than in their home countries.[15] Jewish immigrants in the United States more actively celebrate Hanukkah as a substitute for Christmas.[16] English has become a more commonly used language in Sikh *gurdwaras* (temples) in the West.[17]

However, beyond congregational style and religious holidays, immigrants can also adapt their religiosity.[18] Religious attendance is a good indicator of religious change. For instance, Guo Kai Li not only adapted to Canada by belonging to a church, but she also adapted her religious service attendance over time, becoming more like the average Montrealer. Compared to China, where an extremely small share of the population regularly goes to Buddhist temples or Christian churches, Canada is a relatively religiously active place, less religious than the United States, but more religious than most European countries.[19] So it is unsurprising that Guo Kai Li, like other immigrants in Montreal with no religious attendance prior to moving to Canada, would become more religious over time. Simultaneously, however, very religious immigrants in Montreal may lower their religious attendance in bringing their religiosity more in line with the general society.

These parallel movements of immigrants in Montreal from zero to some religious attendance and others with high to lower religious attendance are undergoing the same process of religious adaptation. Each situation is creating a group of immigrants that, on average, is moving toward the religiosity levels of the general public in their local area. In fact, actual religious attendance backs this up. In 2001, a sample of new immigrants to Canada was asked about their religious attendance. When the percentages of immigrants attending religious services regularly are lined up with religious attendance for the general public by Canadian city (see figure 2.1), there is no distinctive pattern or obvious connection between immigrants and the general public. For example, the most religious immigrants do not live in the cities where the general population is the most religious. An obvious example in 2001 is immigrants in the city of Kitchener, where only 2 percent of immigrants attended religious services weekly or more often, but over a quarter of the general public attended weekly or more frequently.

But these religious-attendance rate gaps between immigrant and general-public religious attendance in Canadian cities start to close only two years later. In 2003, immigrants were again asked about their religious attendance, and a pattern emerged. On average, some of Canada's most religious cities (see Windsor and Abbotsford) also contained some of Canada's most religious immigrants. Vice versa, some of Canada's least religious cities (see Montreal and Quebec City) contained some of Canada's least religious immigrants. The immigrant/general public match-up by Canadian city is not perfect. Kitchener, for example, is still not as aligned as Windsor or Abbotsford. But on average, immigrants do seem to religiously adapt, moving closer to average attendance levels of the general public in their city over time.

Just as immigrants to Canada, like Guo Kai Li, seem to religiously adapt to their local surroundings, religious attendance should also occur at a country level. If religious adaptation is occurring, frequency of religious attendance among immigrants living longer in the country should be closer to the total population average compared with immigrants

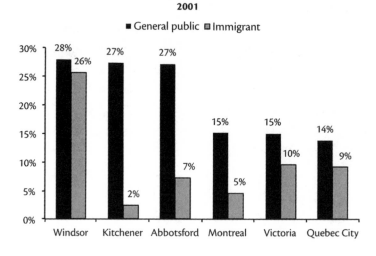

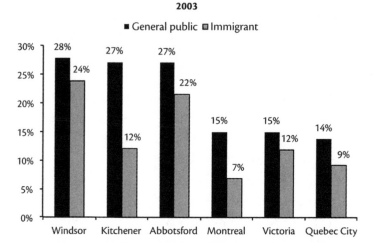

Figure 2.1. Percentage attending religious services weekly or more by
Canadian city. (Longitudinal Survey of Immigrants to Canada 2001, 2003;
General Social Surveys 2001–2005)

living in the country for less time. For example, there is a slight increase
in attending religious services monthly or more from 31 percent of non-
Christian immigrants living in the United States ten years or less to 35
percent of those living in the United States more than ten years.[20] So
the religious attendance of non-Christian immigrants appears to be

adapting, becoming more like the American population, whose monthly-or-more religious attendance is more than 40 percent. In other words, non-Christian immigrants in the United States, who start out as moderately religious, become more religious over time, becoming more like religious Americans.

Adaptation also seems to be happening in Canada and Western Europe. Christian immigrants in both contexts drop their religious attendance over time, slowly converging to the lower religious attendance levels in the total population. A similar decline in immigrant religious attendance in Canada is happening among other religious groups as well.

Therefore, religious adaptation seems to be happening, at least for most immigrants. After a period of disruption in their religious patterns, immigrants begin, on average, to resemble the new country's population, becoming more or less religious over time, depending on the national and local context. Evidence for this faith adaptation is strongest when one looks at religious attendance; but traditions, ways of organizing religious groups, and even beliefs can also adapt the longer immigrants live in their new country. Although immigrant religious groups are never identical to nonimmigrant religious groups, adjustment toward the general public's religious practice is ongoing.

But this religious adaptation process does not occur for all groups in all places. Upon further examination of attendance for other religion

Table 2.2. Percentage Attending Religious Services Monthly or More by Time in Country and Religion

Immigrant religious group and time in country	United States	Canada	Western Europe
Total population	42%	32%	21%
Christian immigrants—10 years or less	51%	64%	47%
Christian immigrants—more than 10 years	52%	**50%**	**43%**
Other religion immigrants—10 years or less	31%	56%	42%
Other religion immigrants—more than 10 years	35%	51%	42%

Sources: U.S.: General Social Survey 2004 (total population); New Immigrant Survey 2003 (immigrant). Canada: Ethnic Diversity Survey 2003. Western Europe: European Social Survey 2002–2010.

Note: Bold type indicates significant differences for time in country (by religious group) within a 95 percent confidence interval.

immigrants in Europe, most of whom are Muslim, there is less change. About four in ten Muslim immigrants attend religious services monthly or more, regardless of whether they've been in the country for five, ten, or more years. By contrast, only two in ten Europeans attend religious services at least once a month, about half the rate of immigrant Muslims. Unlike immigrant religious groups in Canada and the United States, immigrant Muslims in Western Europe do not seem to be religiously adapting. Something unique is happening with Muslim immigrants in Europe. Perhaps the stability in religious attendance among Muslim immigrants is due to unique circumstances in Europe, or some kind of barrier that keeps Muslims from adapting like other religious groups.

Do Immigrants Religiously React to Changes in Society?

In the late nineteenth and early twentieth centuries, America's economy was growing fast and needed more workers. Responding to the call, several million migrants from Eastern Europe, Ireland, and Italy moved to the United States. However, with the arrival of migrant workers from Europe, a new type of immigrant was entering the United States. Unlike Northern Europeans before them, this group was not Protestant. Instead, it was Catholic, holding strange religious traditions and customs (at least to those in America at the time) while claiming allegiance to a foreign religious authority—the Vatican.[21]

Although Catholics are considered part of American mainstream society today, this was not the case when they first landed on America's shores. Nativists considered Catholics less than Christian, inferior, and outright unpatriotic. According to several Americans' perspectives, Catholic immigrants would never fully integrate into American society.[22]

Given this hostility, some Americans may have expected Catholic immigrants to downplay their religious attachments or maybe even convert to Protestant denominations. Although some did this, most did not. In fact, the lack of welcome for their religious traditions provided

Catholic immigrants to the United States an opportunity to showcase their religious identity even more.

Although these Catholic immigrants were somewhat religious in their home country, there was even greater reason to be religious once they arrived in the United States. Not only was the United States a fairly religious country to begin with (recall religious adaptation, explained earlier) but because of the ridicule many Catholics received during their arrival, their religious identity became sacred—an identity that could not be lost in further generations. This led Catholic immigrants to build Catholic institutions like local parishes and parochial schools, as well as ethnic and community organizations. In the face of opposition, Catholicism thrived in these immigrant communities, a sort of reaction to the pressures of religious conformity.

In becoming more religious, Catholics also became more American. Will Herberg, in his classic book *Protestant, Catholic, and Jew,* describes it this way:

> Of the immigrant who came to this country it was expected that, sooner or later, either in his own person or through his children, he will give up virtually everything he had brought with him from the "old country"—his language, his nationality, his manner of life—and will adopt the ways of his new home. Within broad limits, however, his becoming American did not involve his abandoning the old religion in favor of some native American substitute. Quite the contrary, not only was he expected to retain his old religion, as he was not expected to retain his old language or nationality, but such was the shape of America that it was largely in and through his religion that he, or rather his children and grandchildren, found an identifiable place in American life.[23]

Although it is difficult to trace whether Catholic immigrants in the United States became religious because they were adapting to a religious America or because they were reacting to the hostility shown to them for being Catholic or a combination of both, it cannot be denied that for immigrants arriving to the United States around the turn of the twentieth century, religious identity was important. For the United States, it was the first time when a distinctly different religious group grew to such large numbers. Given the sheer number of Catholic immigrants, it was America's largest experience with religious pluralism.

Even Guo Kai Li in Montreal had a similar experience. Despite Canada's Christian tradition, the country has become increasingly secular in recent years, both in its government and in its general population. As each generation comes of age, fewer and fewer are attending religious activities, and faith is rarely discussed. And when it is brought up, it is often with disdain, considered a relic of the past—much the way Guo Kai Li's family in China spoke of religion. So even though Guo Kai Li became a member of a Christian church in a place where Christians had lived for decades, she felt the need for a deeper faith, somewhat driven by the public hostility she felt around her. Her faith was strengthened in the face of opposition. It became more real when her religious convictions felt threatened.[24]

This type of religious reaction requires several conditions. First, the religious group needs to be of a certain size and concentration, not too small to go unnoticed but also not too geographically scattered to avoid public view.[25] Second, religion must be a bright boundary line that distinguishes a new religious group from the majority religious group. This boundary line can be social or it can also be legal with some kind of governmental preference for the majority religious group.[26] Third, the immigrant religious group must experience a less than happy welcome from the general public. The reasons for this hostility can be many. But as the immigrant religious group feels threatened, its religious identity and thus its religious traditions become more, not less, important.[27]

Move forward a century to Western Europe, and an experience somewhat similar to the Catholic story in the United States has developed. Following the Second World War, Europe needed workers to help them rebuild their economies. Several thousands from Muslim-majority countries like Turkey, Morocco, and Algeria accepted Europe's invitation. But much to the surprise of Europeans, these Muslim migrants stayed, bringing family members and raising their children in some of Europe's largest cities. More Muslims came as Europe's economy took off during the 1990s. Today, Europe now has more than twelve million Muslim immigrants, and several million more than that when children of immigrants are included.[28]

As seen in earlier survey data, these Muslim immigrants don't follow the pattern of religious adaptation seen among other religious groups in the United States. For example, while Christian immigrants living longer in the United Kingdom and France have lower religious attendance than Christian immigrants living in these same countries for fewer years, Muslim religious attendance has remained constant or has increased over time. For example, about three in ten Muslim immigrants living in Germany ten years or less attend religious services at least once a month. Four in ten Muslim immigrants living in Germany for more than ten years attend at similar levels. With fewer than two in ten Germans attending monthly or more frequently, this high level of religiosity among Muslim immigrants stands out, especially when it appears that their religious commitment grows over time. In fact, as will be shown in chapter 4, religious attendance among Muslims remains high even among children of immigrants.

Table 2.3. Percentage Attending Religious Services Monthly or More by Time in Country and Religion

Immigrant religious group and time in country	United Kingdom	Germany	France
Total population	15%	14%	5%
Christian immigrants—10 years or less	56%	20%	37%
Christian immigrants—more than 10 years	**49%**	25%	**28%**
Muslim immigrants—10 years or less	57%	32%	17%
Muslim immigrants—more than 10 years	**62%**	**43%**	**21%**

Sources: UK: Understanding Society Survey 2009. Germany: Gender and Generations Survey 2005. France: Trajectoires et Origines Survey 2007.

Note: Bold type indicates significant differences for time in country (by religious group) within a 95 percent confidence interval.

What explains this heightened religiosity? Many factors could explain it, but it could be a religious reaction. With several wars in Muslim countries, the events of September 11th, and conversations in Europe criticizing Muslim traditions like crowded mosques and women wearing head coverings, Muslims may feel threatened.[29]

Additional survey data provide some evidence of this religious reaction.[30] The European Social Survey is administered in several European countries every two years. The total populations of these countries are surveyed, including interviews with both immigrants and nonimmigrants. When Muslim immigrants are separated from the rest of the population, we can compare their average level of religious attendance against all kinds of variables. To see if hostility toward immigrants is associated with higher levels of religious attendance among Muslims, we can compare the percentage regularly attending religious services by region of residence with the general public's attitudes toward immigrants.[31]

Indeed, Muslim immigrants are the most religious in regions where

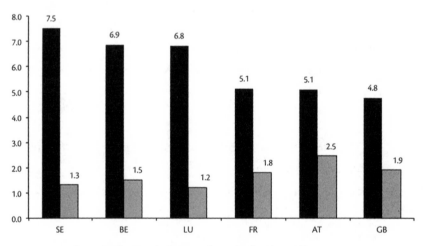

Figure 2.2. Immigrant receptivity and immigrant Muslim religious attendance by European regions within selected European countries. (European Social Survey 2002, 2004, 2006, and 2008)

the population is the most hostile toward immigrants. For example, where attitudes toward immigrants are the least welcoming in regions within France, Austria, and Great Britain, Muslim religious attendance is highest. By contrast, where attitudes toward immigrants are more welcoming, in regions like Sweden, Belgium, and Luxembourg, Muslim religious attendance is much lower.

Hostility toward an immigrant religious group seems to lead to a situation where the immigrant group does not follow the normal path of religious adaptation. In other words, an immigrant religious group may feel threatened, and in response, only become more religiously committed. So it appears that being Muslim in today's Europe, Catholic in early-twentieth-century America, or even, like Guo Kai Li, a new Christian in Canada is an unwavering identity.

Do Immigrants Change Their Religions?

When Guo Kai Li was contemplating a shift from atheism to Christianity, it was not a quick decision. As she became more familiar with the Bible and the people in her church group, she had to first be convinced there was a god. Then she had to determine whether the god her church group was worshipping was indeed for her. The process took several months before she came to a point of decision.

Switching from one religion to another is often a long process.[32] And there are costs to switching religions: new friends to make, more time invested in religious activities, and a new way of life to learn. Probably the greatest sacrifice is relationships with family and friends. Those closest to the immigrant may be opposed to the change, so switching religions can mean losing people in an immigrant's life.

Guo Kai Li understood the dangers of becoming a Christian. But in her situation, the risks were minimal. She discussed it with her husband and he was fine with the idea. (He actually saw his wife's faith as a plus in their adjustment to Canada.) And although Guo Kai Li knew that some of her family in China would find it strange, they weren't physically near her, and she could share details in her own time and on her own terms. Although nervous about it at first, Guo Kai Li grew more and more comfortable with the idea of becoming a Christian. In some ways, she saw it as an opportunity to recapture her roots, following in the footsteps of her Christian grandmother.

Guo Kai Li's story, however, is not the norm. She had adapted to Canadian culture, becoming more religious in Canada than in her native China. But an outright change in religious groups is more the exception than the rule. For example, immigrants in the United States receiving their green cards in 2003 were interviewed a few months after becoming permanent residents and again five years later. In each interview, they were asked for their religion. In the first interview, they were also asked the religious group they had been part of as a child. The results are shown in table 2.4.[33]

People move into a religion and move out again, so it is difficult to know which immigrant religions are net gainers. However, one useful comparison is retention rates or the percentage of immigrants staying in a religious group. Since we are dealing with the same people over two different time points, retention rates (bold figures in table 2.4) in this survey of immigrants cannot increase; they can only stay the same or go down.

Religions experiencing some of the lowest retention rates following migration are Christian groups, Buddhists, and those with no religion. But, these retention rates are still relatively high, meaning that only a small percentage of immigrants is switching to a different religious group. For example, of new immigrants to the United States raised Catholic, nearly nine in ten (88 percent) were still Catholic after they became permanent residents. Protestant and Christian Orthodox immigrants have similar retention rates, while immigrants raised Buddhist or with no religious affiliation have slightly lower retention rates. Meanwhile, almost all immigrants raised Hindu or Muslim continued to practice these religions when becoming permanent residents.

Five years later, retention rates are even higher among these new immigrants to the United States. Almost all immigrants who were

Table 2.4. Religious Distribution of U.S. Immigrants by Migration and Time in Country

Religion at time of permanent residency	Religion raised						
	Catholic	Orthodox	Protestant	Muslim	Buddhist	Hindu	No religion
Catholic	**88%**	0%	2%	0%	3%	0%	1%
Christian Orthodox	1%	**91%**	0%	0%	2%	0%	3%
Protestant	5%	3%	**90%**	0%	0%	0%	8%
Muslim	0%	0%	0%	**96%**	0%	0%	0%
Buddhist	0%	0%	0%	0%	**82%**	0%	2%
Hindu	0%	0%	0%	0%	0%	**99%**	0%
No religion	5%	4%	6%	4%	10%	1%	**85%**
Total	100%	100%	100%	100%	100%	100%	100%
Religion 5 years after permanent residency	Religion at time of permanent residency						
	Catholic	Orthodox	Protestant	Muslim	Buddhist	Hindu	No religion
Catholic	**96%**	2%	1%	0%	1%	0%	3%
Christian Orthodox	2%	**92%**	3%	0%	1%	0%	3%
Protestant	2%	3%	**91%**	1%	1%	0%	4%
Muslim	0%	0%	0%	**96%**	0%	0%	0%
Buddhist	0%	0%	0%	0%	**94%**	1%	1%
Hindu	0%	0%	0%	0%	0%	**99%**	0%
No religion	0%	1%	3%	0%	3%	0%	**88%**
Total	100%	100%	100%	100%	100%	100%	100%

Source: New Immigrant Survey 2003.

Note: Bold type indicates retention rates.

Catholic, Muslim, Buddhist, or Hindu when receiving permanent residency were still part of these religious groups five years later. Meanwhile, a small degree of religious change during these five years occurred for immigrants entering the United States as Protestant, Christian Orthodox, and with no religion. For these groups, about one in ten people switched to a different religion.

To which religious groups did these religious switchers who were once Christian or had no religion go? Departing Catholics became Protestant or no longer claimed a religion. Those starting with no religion also became mostly Christian (Catholic or Protestant). Many immigrants moving away from Protestantism ended up with no religion. But again, this movement between religious groups is the minority experience. In no instance did more than 10 percent of a given religious group switch religions in the five years after receiving a green card. And only a slightly higher percentage (12 percent) of immigrants with no religion became affiliated with a religion five years later.

This relative lack of religious change agrees with Will Herberg's idea mentioned earlier. Immigrants in the United States become more American by becoming strongly attached to their religious group, regardless of whether the group is part of the religious majority. In fact, immigrants are rarely expected to change religious groups. Even though it occurs for a small minority, there are no huge shifts in religious affiliation, even over time. If shifts do occur, they are more likely to happen before migration, not after. And in the limited number of instances where faith changes after a move, the general direction is toward Protestantism, America's historic majority religion, especially for immigrants with no religious affiliation in the first place.[34]

What about other countries? Are immigrants more likely to change religious groups in other places? A survey of immigrants from France provides some clues. Although immigrants were not surveyed a second time after migrating as they were in the United States, information about changes occurring over the immigrant's lifetime, whether before or after migration, is available. Similar to the story in the United States, the religious breakdown of immigrants in France is about the same as in their childhood. Retention rates (bold figures in table 2.5) for religious groups are also similar to those in the United States, with large declines for Buddhist immigrants (presumably before migration, as in the U.S. data) and moderate declines for other religious groups, including those with no religion. However, unlike in the United States, religious switches generally move toward no religious affiliation. This makes sense since the dominant religious group in France is no religion.[35]

So was Guo Kai Li's experience in Canada also a rare event? In light of the data from the United States and France, that appears to be somewhat the case. However, religious retention rates can be higher for some ethnic groups than for others. A recent study using Canadian census data does find a slight shift over time toward Christianity

Table 2.5. Religious Distribution of Immigrants in France

Religion today	Religion raised				
	Christian	Muslim	Buddhist	Other religion	No religion
Christian	**85%**	0%	4%	5%	8%
Muslim	0%	**91%**	0%	0%	5%
Buddhist	0%	0%	**74%**	0%	2%
Other religion	1%	0%	1%	**76%**	0%
No religion	14%	8%	21%	17%	**84%**
Total	100%	100%	100%	100%	100%

Source: Trajectoires et Origines Survey 2007.

Note: Bold type indicates retention rates.

among Chinese immigrants claiming no religion compared with the year when they first arrived.[36] Again, the movement is not huge, but it is notable. So it looks like Guo Kai Li was among the minority of Chinese immigrants, many of whom entered North America with no religious affiliation, who have made a similar religious change in Canada. But the majority reflects Zhang Yi's experience, entering Canada with no religion and keeping this faith (or lack thereof) while adjusting to Canadian culture.[37]

From the evidence on hand, religious switching is not that common among immigrants. It may occur in some groups more than others, particularly among Christians and those with no religion, but it is still a relatively rare event. When it does happen, the net movement is toward the majority or the most prominent religious group in the immigrant's new country. For example, Protestants in the United States seem to gain most from religious switching while it is the no-religion group that experiences the greatest net gains in France. In Canada, as seen in Guo Kai Li's and Zhang Yi's lives, it is possible that both directions of switching are happening at the same time, especially when current reality doesn't always match religious tradition. For example, some immigrants in Canada, like Guo Kai Li, are becoming Christian in a culture that is historically Christian. But others, like Zhang Yi, gravitate toward no religion, a growing religious (or nonreligious) identity in Canada's general public.

A Changed Faith or a Faith Change?

There is no doubt that an immigrant's faith changes after he or she moves to a new country. But how does it change? First, the act of moving to a new country disrupts the religious patterns of immigrants. As an immigrant adjusts in the early days to his or her new home, finding a religious group may not always be the highest priority. But the disruption can be even greater, perhaps for the immigrant's entire lifetime. In fact, an immigrant may never be as religious as he or she was in the home country.[38]

But once the initial shock of migrating is over and the immigrant starts adjusting to the new home, religion usually comes back into the mix. In this phase, immigrants will adapt their religious practices to the society around them, including how frequently they attend religious gatherings. This adaptation happens both at national and local levels. And although immigrants may never look religiously the same as the general public, they are over time changing their religious habits as they become more aligned with the general population. Both in the disruption of immigrant religious attendance and the adaptation of attendance to the society around them, immigrants are experiencing a changed faith.

However, this adaptation doesn't occur for all groups. In particular, Muslims in Western Europe seem to maintain high levels of religiosity, perhaps even increasing their religious commitment over time. Evidence points to the possibility of a religious reaction among Muslims in Europe. With the high levels of hostility Muslim immigrants feel from the general public, their religious identity grows stronger, leading to higher religiosity. In this way, their faith is also changing, but not in the expected direction found among immigrant religious groups adapting to their new countries. Nonetheless, this reaction to hostility is yet another example of a changed faith compared with their experiences in their home country.

All these changes are examples of a changing faith—a faith that is shifting over time—but not a complete switching of faith. Although the example of Guo Kai Li indicates a faith change, it is more the exception than the rule for most immigrants. Yes, Guo Kai Li was becoming more religiously active, changing her religious commitment from zero to something. This is an expected adjustment when living in a relatively more religious Canada compared to a less religious China. But a faith change from no religion to Christianity is not the norm for most immigrants. In this way, the lack of change in faith is better identified with Zhang Yi, Guo Kai Li's husband. His story more closely resembles the unchanging faith of immigrants.

A faith that moves with migrants can move all the way around the world. But that faith never remains quite the same after the move. It is disrupted, adapted, possibly reactive, but in the end is most likely the same faith, at least in name. But as an immigrant's faith is in the process of change, so is everything else in his or her life—relationships, health, career, and citizenship. Where does faith figure into these other aspects of an immigrant's life? Is religion a help or hindrance in the way immigrants integrate into society?

3

Integrating Faith

Everyone in Mohammed's family knew he was a go-getter. He was the first child in his family to do everything, even though he had older siblings. He was the first to tie his shoes. The first to go to the mosque by himself. The first to complete high school. The first to leave Morocco.

Yes, once Mohammed completed his dual-language (French and Arabic) high school education, he decided to make the journey north to France. Knowing he wanted to pursue more education so he could fulfill his lifelong dream of building airplanes, he decided that southern France would provide the most opportunity.[1] Airbus's factory was in Toulouse, so being there might give him the opportunity to at least work as a parts technician someday. After receiving a work visa through his uncle's grocery market, he got on a plane bound for France (again a first for his family).[2]

As the plane shot across the runway and up into the air, Mohammed's mind also soared. He imagined himself building parts for the same Airbus 320 he was now flying in. What a great life he was going to have! Not only would he someday have the opportunity to work his dream job, but his future kids would have a much better life than he did. As the plane descended into Toulouse, he spotted neighborhood after neighborhood of small cottages on the outskirts of the city. He imagined himself living in one of the small cottages, married, with a couple of kids, enjoying the good life.

Toulouse was not as bustling as Mohammed's home city of Casablanca, but it was still interesting to him. There were historical monuments, museums, libraries, and of course the occasional test flight by Airbus over the city. But all those things were secondary; Mohammed was a busy guy. He worked six days a week in his uncle's grocery store, stocking the shelves, taking orders from seniors, and managing *la caisse* (the cash register). Each evening, he spent several hours reading French literature, doing math exercises, doing anything to improve his chances of entering college the following year. After all his hard work, he was granted that opportunity. He became a student at a technical college not too far from his uncle's grocery store.

Mohammed graduated two years later with a diploma in aerospace engineering. The degree title sounded better than it really was, but it would be enough for him to get a job at one of Airbus's parts distributors somewhere around Toulouse. Mohammed sent resumé after resumé after resumé to posted jobs that matched his qualifications. After thirty resumés, he had only one interview. And that job went to a Christian classmate from Cameroon. Mohammed was thoroughly disappointed. Here he was a trained technician, but no matter how hard he tried, no jobs were open to him. And the French economy was at its peak. What was happening? He heard about other Muslim men in his class having trouble finding a job. By comparison, every non-Muslim in his class had a job within a couple of months of graduating.

After a few more months of job hunting, Mohammed's uncle convinced him to give up on his dream to build airplanes and instead open his own business. His uncle had a little extra space at the back of the store where he could set up a lunch counter. Perhaps Mohammed could serve up some of his Moroccan specialties. Both the North African and the French students at Mohammed's former college raved about his authentic *tajine* and *merguez* sausage. So with no further luck in the job market, Mohammed reluctantly set up his business. It was a hard start, but within a couple of years, he had built up a loyal clientele that paid the bills. His lunch counter wasn't going to make him rich. Nor would it help him fulfill his dream to build airplanes or live in a cottage outside of the city. But at least it was a job, much more than many other Muslim men his age had.

Working every morning, afternoon, and evening, Mohammed hardly had time to go to the mosque. But when he did, it seemed as if all of his troubles were a distant memory. Praying at the mosque reminded him of home, giving him peace about his job situation. Unfortunately, he didn't have time to stay and socialize after Friday prayers. He always had to rush back to his restaurant to serve the after-mosque crowd. But he did get to know some Moroccans who came to his restaurant. One day, he met Fatima, a young woman also from Morocco. She went to a prestigious college in the city and was finishing a four-year degree in politics. Her dream was to be a lawyer. Mohammed liked Fatima's independent spirit. Fatima liked Mohammed's gentle and kind heart. Mohammed and Fatima married when she completed her politics degree.

But before Fatima started law school, the couple had their first child. Family became more important, so Fatima never fulfilled her dream to become a lawyer. Instead she established a community organization that helped abused women access medical and legal help. With this organization, she became a highly respected person in Toulouse.

How Can Immigrant Faith Help or Hinder Immigrant Integration?

Immigrants don't always have it easy. They are often dealing with a new culture, a new language, and new surroundings. The process of integrating into the new country's society is not short-lived. Sometimes it can take years or even generations to become fully part of the new society.

Immigrant adjustment, often called immigrant integration, has a long history of study.[3] To see whether immigrants are improving their social and economic standing in the new country, researchers often compare immigrants to the general public with no migration background. Sometimes ethnic groups (white versus nonwhite, Asian versus European) are compared with each other. Studies focus on a range of immigrant outcomes in evaluating whether an immigrant group is successfully making it in society. And although not all residents of the immigrant's new country may expect immigrants to integrate in every way, especially their cultural and religious heritage, there is often the expectation that new immigrants eventually communicate in the country's language, participate in the local economy, and in time become contributing members of society.[4]

Many integration studies take into account differences in language ability, education, and other factors that may lead one immigrant group to have a different experience than another immigrant group. For example, immigrants arriving with low education may have a more difficult time advancing in their careers than immigrants with high education. Rarely, however, is religion studied as an important aspect of immigrant integration. Nonetheless, there is evidence that religion can make a world of difference for many immigrant groups.

For example, religious organizations can offer a spiritual and emotional refuge for immigrants, offering them an ethnic community that reminds them of home and makes them feel comfortable in the midst of all the chaos happening in their lives. Churches, mosques, temples, and other worship centers also offer resources for immigrants. Many of these religious centers have classes to help immigrants improve their language skills, understand the new country's culture, or obtain new skills like writing a resumé or preparing for a job interview. Religious organizations also offer a setting for networking with other immigrants and sometimes with nonimmigrants. Consequently, these congregations present opportunities for people to share job leads, obtain job referrals from co-congregants, or learn how to work through bureaucratic red tape. Immigrant religious organizations also depend on volunteers. These volunteer roles can boost the self-confidence of immigrants and provide a way for them to gain greater respect in their ethnic community as well as society at large.[5]

In these ways, religion can be a bridge for immigrants adjusting to a new place. For instance, going to the mosque provided Mohammed some solace in an otherwise precarious job situation. It helped him focus on things that were familiar, and also gave him the opportunity to pray for help during his time of need. Although his employment situation did not seem to improve, praying did help him come to terms with the situation as he remembered that his predicament was in Allah's hands.

But religion also seemed to be a barrier for Mohammed as he adjusted to French society. He was Muslim and there was little he could do to change that. He had a Muslim-sounding name, had darker skin than most people in France, and lived in a predominantly immigrant (and mostly Muslim) neighborhood. All these things about his background alerted potential employers not only to his North African heritage but also to his religious convictions. Could it be that being Muslim somehow blocked his dream of becoming an aerospace engineer? Were people not hiring him because he was Muslim?

Religion can help immigrants, but it can also hinder their adjustment. Whether religion is a help or hindrance depends on where immigrants settle.

For example, the American general public is fairly religious. The United States also separates church from state. By contrast, Europeans have become less religious in recent years, yet may still maintain some kind of connection to religion, especially since many European countries have a state religion.

These different religious contexts can make for profound differences in the way immigrants use religion to psychologically adapt in the new country, succeed economically, and become full members of society. In a broad comparison, there seem to be major differences in the way religion can help or hinder immigrants in the United States compared with Europe. For instance, some migration scholars describe religion as a bridge for incorporation into American society, while it is a barrier for integrating into European society.[6]

In the United States, religion can have a bridging effect for immigrant adjustment. American society has had centuries of experience with immigration, and more specifically with religious minorities. Consequently, new religious groups are not threatening to American society, especially when their number is not large. America's legal structure also allows for separation of religion and state, not favoring one religious group over another. Though religion is prominent within public conversation and U.S. politics, people are free to worship or not to worship in the manner they choose. In this way, immigrants of all faith backgrounds have equal opportunity to participate in America's religious landscape, with no religious group receiving extra benefits or special favoritism by the state. Also, the bulk of immigrants in the United States are Christians who share the same faith as the general public. This means that any negative view of immigrants in the United States is not seen through a religious lens but by other filters like race (Hispanic, black) or language (Spanish-speaking).[7] All these factors can make it relatively easier to be a religious minority in the United States, not only in socially adjusting to a new place but also in receiving equal treatment on the job market.

Immigrant faith in the United States can also serve as a bridge in other ways. The U.S. general public is fairly religious, at least compared to the general population of most European countries.[8] Religion is an important part of many Americans' lives, and it is one of the most enduring ways a newcomer can get involved in the community.[9] Also, religious congregations in the United States are not only places to worship, but they can also operate as community centers, offering their members help in whatever way they can. This organizational model of religion in the United States can assist immigrants in finding jobs, advancing their careers, or simply helping with their cultural adjustment.

By contrast, in Europe, religion can be a barrier for immigrant adjustment. Europe has a long historical tradition of mixing faith and state together. Many countries have official religions.[10] These Christian state religions can make it difficult for religious minorities to be officially recognized, especially since many European countries have received large numbers of immigrants only in recent years. Also, the general population is skeptical that these religious minorities can effectively integrate into European society.[11] Added to this fact, nearly half of immigrants in Europe are Muslim—a religious minority in Europe.[12] So, unlike Americans, Europeans often view immigrants first in religious terms, not by their origins or language. All these factors can make faith, particularly for religious minorities, a hindrance for successful adjustment into European society.

Additionally, Europe's religious system is less congregational. Not only is a growing share of Europe's population not going to church anymore, but the organizational structure is largely designed to enable worship rites, not to create community centers as in the United States. Thus, there are fewer opportunities for immigrants to lean on religious organizations to help them find their way in European society. If anything, overtly religious immigrants in an increasingly secular society in Europe could be met with a negative public perception, and their overt religious affiliation could possibly hinder, more than help, their integration.

Although Mohammed lived in France, his experience could have almost as easily occurred in almost any other Western European country. Many comparisons noting the role of religion for immigrant integration find more similarities than differences, particularly among immigrant religious minorities.[13] Mohammed's Islamic faith, which possibly hindered his adjustment to France, could have helped him if he had migrated to the United States instead. In France, the high number of Muslim immigrants, combined with the general public's view that Muslims are very religious people, makes for a less welcoming environment for Muslims in an otherwise secular France. Studies in Europe have demonstrated that Muslim immigrants and their children cannot access employment because of a combination of their Muslim-sounding names, their birthplaces, and their addresses in predominantly North African neighborhoods.[14] If Mohammed had lived in the United States, it is possible that religious discrimination would be less of a problem, at least in getting a job for which he was qualified.

Western Europe and the United States are two extremes of immigrant societies where religion plays either a hindering (Europe) or helping (United States) role for immigrant integration. But not all countries fall so neatly into this categorization. Canada, for example, provides a middle case where elements of both the American and the European contexts are simultaneously present.[15] For example, Canada has a legal separation of church and state like the United States, but has had a history of privileging Christian denominations in providing social services. Also, immigrants in Canada are religiously diverse—less Christian than immigrants in the United States, but not comprising such a large share of religious minorities (and specifically Muslims) as found in most Western European countries. Consequently, Canadians speak of both religious and ethnic diversity when they think about immigrants. Also, Canada is not an entirely irreligious or overly religious society. It has more of the congregational model of worship found in the United States where immigrants can potentially access resources to help them adjust. But Canadians are generally less religiously active in these organizations than Americans, though not as inactive as Europeans. In these ways, immigrant faith could be both a barrier for religious minorities in Canada and a bridge as immigrants of any faith rely on their religious communities to help their adjustment.

Regardless of whether religion is a barrier or a bridge for immigrant adjustment, faith does not operate in the same way for all immigrants in all places. Being a Muslim may have employment consequences in France, but it may make no difference in the United States. Being religious may make immigrants in almost every country feel more comfortable in their new surroundings, but it may only help them economically in places where religious congregations are an active part of society. Whatever the case, immigrant faith cannot be easily described as a help or hindrance. It depends on the immigrant religious group and where it has settled. The role of religion also depends on the type of integration—psychological, economic, or social.[16] The remainder of this chapter looks at each form of integration separately, describing how the experience can vary by religious group, but also by the immigrant's context.

Does Immigrant Faith Help Immigrants Psychologically Integrate?

When Mohammed worked in his uncle's grocery and later when he was a student, he made it a point to go to Friday prayers at the local mosque whenever possible. He went to the mosque slightly more often in Morocco. (It helped that all businesses in Casablanca shut down on Friday during prayer time.) But even though it took more effort to go to the mosque in Toulouse, he found it much more meaningful than in Casablanca.

When he gathered with other Muslims at the mosque, he felt a peace in the midst of the daily chaos he experienced in France. Not only was he busy studying and working, but he also didn't always know how to react to people in France. He knew the language, but he didn't always feel comfortable engaging them outside of the classroom or inside his uncle's store. Also, many of the values held by most people living in France were different from those taught to him. For example, it was nothing for a French man his age to enjoy a glass or two of wine at dinner—something Mohammed would never consider doing. Some French women would sometimes wear little clothing during the summer, especially at the beach. Again, this was something his family would consider improper. The mosque offered a literal sanctuary from the outside, French world. At the conclusion of his prayer time, he could breathe more easily, laugh with other Muslim men in the nearby courtyard, and for a moment feel like he was back home in Morocco.

In France, Mohammed listened more intently to the imam's sermons. As a boy, he had found the imam's sermons in Morocco boring, but now they held greater meaning. The imam talked about Allah in ways that were more real for him and his situation. When things got rough, Mohammed recited Quaranic verses that talked about Allah's protection for his followers. When things went well, he thanked Allah for the blessings of life. As an immigrant, he found that religion brought much more meaning to life, especially when things did not go as expected.[17]

The emotional stress and mental tension immigrants experience can produce high levels of anxiety.[18] This anxiety is due not only to a changing employment situation but also to cultural change. Immigrants don't always know how to process these changes, leading to high levels of depression among some immigrants. Also, many immigrants search for ways to reconcile value differences they see in the new country compared with their home countries.[19]

The comfort and reassurance Mohammed experienced in going to the mosque is similar to the stories of immigrants involved in other religious congregations, both in the United States and in Europe. For example, a study of Haitian immigrants in Miami, Montreal, and Paris showed that Catholic Haitians in all three countries regularly used their faith to help them emotionally survive in their new countries. Without their faith, their lives would have had more turmoil and unrest. Many spoke of how they prayed in times of desperation, found emotional relief by attending mass, and sought a deeper understanding of life's challenges by using biblical examples and references.[20]

There are several ways to measure whether religion is a psychological refuge for immigrants. One way is to simply compare whether immigrants regularly attending religious services claim to be happier than those who are not attending religious services. Although Americans who attend religious services are happier than Americans not attending religious services, religious attendance does not seem to make a huge difference for the happiness of immigrants, both Christian and non-Christian, living in the United States.

Differences in happiness by religious attendance are also small in

Table 3.1. Percentage Saying They Are Very Happy

Immigrant religious group and religious attendance	United States	Canada	Western Europe
General public	88%	77%	55%
Attending, general public	**91%**	**81%**	55%
Nonattending, general public	86%	75%	56%
Attending, Christian immigrants	80%	76%	55%
Nonattending, Christian immigrants	81%	79%	56%
Attending, other religion immigrants	86%	**80%**	**52%**
Nonattending, other religion immigrants	87%	72%	47%

Sources: U.S.: General Social Survey 2000–2010. Canada: Canada General Social Survey 2008. Western Europe: European Social Survey 2002–2010.

Note: Attending = monthly or more often; nonattending = less than once a month or not at all. Bold type indicates significant differences for attending and nonattending individuals within a 95 percent confidence interval. General public is native-born.

Europe, especially for Christian immigrants. However, more than half of immigrants belonging to other religions (mostly Islam) in Western Europe and attending religious services monthly or more often describe themselves as very happy whereas less than half of immigrants belonging to the same religious groups yet attending less frequently claim to be very happy.

Canada seems to follow a similar pattern as Europe. A greater percentage of immigrants belonging to other religions and attending religious services regularly is very happy compared with those who attend less frequently. From these statistics, religion seems to be associated with happier immigrants in places where religion is said to be more of a barrier for religious minorities, as in Europe and Canada. By contrast, religious service attendance does not seem to be correlated with happier Christian immigrants in any context. It is possible that some of the cultural and economic challenges facing immigrants belonging to religious minorities in contexts where religion is said to be a barrier for integration lead these religious groups more than others to find psychological relief by being involved in their religious communities.

But self-described happiness is a rather subjective measure of emotional relief or lack of mental stress. A more scientific approach is to examine incidence rates of immigrant depression as associated with religious attendance. In a recent study of immigrant data in the United States, Australia, and Europe, several measures indicating psychological depression were compared across varying levels of religious attendance.[21] Regardless of religious affiliation (Christian, non-Christian), immigrants attending religious services were on the whole less likely to be depressed or have poor mental and emotional health compared with immigrants not attending religious services. By contrast, involvement in nonreligious groups like ethnic associations or sports leagues was not associated with the same, lower incidence of depression-like symptoms. This indicates that compared with other types of group activity, religious attendance seems to have a unique impact on immigrant mental health.

The study also demonstrated that the positive influence religious attendance has on immigrant mental health is not due simply to happier immigrants being more likely to be part of a religious organization. The study ruled out competing factors, including country origins, time spent in the new country, education levels, and physical health. Also, evidence from Australia showed that immigrants regularly attending religious services after moving to the new country were less likely to experience symptoms of depression when interviewed two years later.

Evidence of immigrant mental health as well as previous analysis on happiness fits with what researchers and sociological observers have said for many years about immigrant religious communities.[22] Immigrants of most religious groups who are actively part of a religious congregation have better mental health and are generally happier than those who are not active in a religious organization. And it appears that this positive emotional effect of religious attendance for immigrants is most pronounced for religious minorities in places where these groups may endure the greatest difficulty.

Does Immigrant Faith Help or Hinder Economic Integration?

Except for refugees and some immigrants joining family members, most people move to a new country for financial reasons. Unemployment, low wages, and low pay for high-level jobs in the country of origin lead people to seek a better life in a new country.

Most immigrants want to succeed and make it economically in the new country.[23] Countries with lots of immigrants also want immigrants to succeed since immigrants make up a growing portion of many countries' workforces. The social and economic success of immigrants can be critical for the growth of economies and stable societies.

Employment

When migrants arrive at their new destinations, often the first priority is to find a job. An immigrant's first job may not be all he or she had hoped for, but some kind of work to make a living is a necessity. Advancement in careers can come later through new opportunities, better language skills, or more education.

As explained earlier, there are few reasons to expect immigrants in the United States will have trouble finding a job because of their religious affiliation. And survey data bear this out. Immigrants of all religious backgrounds (Christians, other religions) are equally as likely to be employed as the American general public. There is slight variation of a percentage point or two depending on whether immigrants regularly attend religious services, but these differences are small, and not statistically significant.[24]

By contrast, employment levels vary considerably between immigrants and nonimmigrants in Europe. More importantly, they also differ by religious group. A slightly lower percentage of Christian immigrants is employed than in the general public, but immigrants belonging to other religions (mostly Islam) are even less likely to be employed. In Europe, the lower employment rates of both Christian and non-Christian immigrants indicate that immigrants overall have more trouble finding a job than Europeans with no migration background. But Christian immigrants still have more success finding a job than immigrants belonging to non-Christian religions.

Table 3.2. Percentage Employed

Immigrant religious group and religious attendance	United States	Canada	Western Europe
General public	94%	98%	94%
Attending, general public	95%	98%	95%
Nonattending, general public	94%	97%	94%
Attending, Christian immigrants	96%	97%	91%
Nonattending, Christian immigrants	95%	97%	90%
Attending, other religion immigrants	95%	95%	86%
Nonattending, other religion immigrants	97%	95%	84%

Sources: U.S.: General Social Survey 2000–2010. Canada: Canada General Social Survey 2004, 2006, 2008, 2009. Western Europe: European Social Survey 2002–2010.

Note: Attending = monthly or more often; nonattending = less than once a month or not at all. Bold type indicates significant differences for attending and nonattending individuals within a 95 percent confidence interval. Samples limited to respondents aged 25–64. General public is native-born.

These employment differences agree with other studies in Europe, particularly for Muslims. Although Europe's Muslims have a lower socio-economic background, lower educational levels, and lower language ability than other immigrant religious groups, Muslims are still less likely to be employed than Christian immigrants or the European general public even when these and other factors are taken into account.[25]

Immigrants belonging to religious minorities in Canada also have a harder time finding a job than the Canadian general public or, for that matter, Christian immigrants living in Canada. Statistics agree. Both attending and nonattending immigrants belonging to non-Christian religions are significantly (in a statistical sense) less employed than the Canadian general public and Christian immigrants living in Canada. Employment levels of religious minorities in Canada may not be as low as those in Europe, but they are still relatively lower than Christian immigrants in Canada and Canadians with no migration background.

Belonging to a religious minority group in Europe and to an extent in Canada is correlated with lower employment. The exact reasons for this are unclear, but these findings agree with the presumption that religion is a barrier for immigrant economic success, at least in finding a job, in places where certain religious groups (mainly Christian) have a historical relationship with the state and where a sizeable number of immigrants in these countries belong to religious minorities.

For a while, Mohammed was one of the jobless immigrants belonging to a religious minority group in Europe. He looked for a job in his area of training for several months. But with the help of his uncle, hard work, and a bit of luck, he became gainfully employed in his own business. Mohammed's religious affiliation as a Muslim may have slowed his employment plans, but it did not result in total unemployment. That said, Mohammed still worked in a job that did not match his qualifications. Could this lack of occupational mobility also be related to being Muslim? Perhaps.

Occupation

Immigrants not only want to find a job, but like anyone else, want to advance in their careers. Due to language and educational challenges, some immigrants never move beyond labor or service jobs. Other immigrants with high levels of education and familiarity with the new country's language may almost immediately find a good job and advance in their careers.

Yet similar to employment, some immigrants belonging to religious minority groups may find it difficult to advance in their careers, especially in contexts like Europe and somewhat in Canada, where belonging to a religious minority group is presumed to be more of a hindrance for economic success.

In Western Europe, more than a quarter of immigrants belonging to non-Christian religions work in professional occupations such as education, science, management, and administration. By contrast, higher percentages of Christian immigrants and the European general public at large work in professional occupations.

Though small, this occupational gap between immigrant religious minorities and Christian immigrants in Europe is somewhat expected. Europe's Muslim immigrants have, on average, less education than

Table 3.3. Percentage Working in a Professional Occupation

Immigrant religious group and religious attendance	United States	Canada	Western Europe
General public	51%	51%	47%
Attending, general public	**56%**	**54%**	48%
Nonattending, general public	47%	51%	47%
Attending, Christian immigrants	37%	52%	32%
Nonattending, Christian immigrants	39%	53%	32%
Attending, other religion immigrants	45%	**47%**	26%
Nonattending, other religion immigrants	63%	54%	30%

Sources: U.S.: General Social Survey 2000–2010. Canada: Canada General Social Survey 2004, 2006, 2008, 2009. Western Europe: European Social Survey 2002–2010.

Note: Attending = monthly or more often; nonattending = less than once a month or not at all. Bold type indicates significant differences for attending and nonattending individuals within a 95 percent confidence interval. Samples limited to employed respondents aged 25–64. General public is native-born.

Christian immigrants. Many of Europe's Muslim immigrants from Turkey and North Africa migrated to work in relatively unskilled jobs. Meanwhile, Christian immigrants from Eastern Europe and the Americas migrated to fill a larger number of skilled jobs. So when other contributing factors like differences in education, time in country, and language ability are factored in, the occupational gap between Christian and religious minority immigrants becomes even smaller.

By contrast, the jobs taken by immigrant religious groups in the United States are much different. On the one hand, most Christian immigrants in the United States are from Latin America, and many of these immigrants are less educated and work in nonprofessional jobs in agriculture, construction, and other services. On the other hand, most immigrants belonging to religious minorities in the United States (a mix of Muslims, Hindus, Buddhists, and other religious groups) have, on average, more education than most Christian immigrants. Consequently, a greater share of immigrants belonging to non-Christian religions in the United States works in professional jobs.

These educational differences between Christian and non-Christian immigrants play out as expected. Less than four in ten Christian immigrants work in professional jobs while about half of the U.S. general public works in similar occupations. Meanwhile, immigrants belonging to other religions work in professional occupations at about the same rate as the U.S. general public. However, when differences in education and socioeconomic background are taken into account, these religious-group differences are mostly erased.[26]

In Canada, though, immigrants belonging to non-Christian religions are not less likely to be employed in a professional job. Around half of religious-minority immigrants, Christian immigrants, *and* the Canadian general public work in professional occupations. In this way, even without additional factors included, there appears to be no religious differences in occupational mobility for immigrants living in Canada.

If belonging to a religious minority group is a barrier to immigrant economic success, the barrier seems to affect finding a job rather than occupational mobility, both in Europe and in Canada.[27] For example, Mohammed's time in a local mosque may have helped his mental state, but it may not have helped his job situation. In fact, it was probably his lack of employment opportunities in France that led him to be more, not less, active in his local mosque. It is difficult to speculate, but if Mohammed had been gainfully employed in a job that matched his education and expertise, he might not have resorted to attending the mosque as frequently. He would have had less time and perhaps less use for emotional solace from the mosque community.

It is also difficult to know how Mohammed's situation could have been different in the United States compared with Europe. Given the statistical evidence, he might have had a better chance of finding a job and perhaps one in his area of training. But it does not appear that involvement in a religious organization in the United States would have significantly helped or hindered his economic success. Somewhat unexpectedly, being part of a religious congregation doesn't seem to provide huge employment dividends or substantial employment challenges to immigrants of any religious group in the United States or Canada.

Does Immigrant Faith Help Immigrants Socially Integrate?

It was not Mohammed's goal to remain hidden from other members of society, whether they were French-born, were from a different ethnic group, belonged to another religion, or spoke different languages than he did. However, it was not always easy for him to become friends with people from different backgrounds. He did not always feel comfortable or know quite what to say to French people.

Robert Putnam describes two types of social interactions between and within groups. The development of these interactions is sometimes labeled "social capital." Bonding social capital is created through interactions with people of a similar background, whether that background is religious, ethnic, or linguistic. By contrast, bridging social capital is created through the interaction between people of different backgrounds.[28]

Table 3.4. Percentage Claiming Contact with Different-Ethnic or Different-Language Friends Monthly or More Often

Immigrant religious group and religious attendance	Different-ethnic friends	Different-language friends
General public	12%	13%
Attending, general public	13%	**15%**
Nonattending, general public	12%	12%
Attending, Christian immigrants	**30%**	40%
Nonattending, Christian immigrants	24%	39%
Attending, other religion immigrants	31%	37%
Nonattending, other religion immigrants	33%	44%

Sources: Canada General Social Survey 2003.

Note: Attending = monthly or more often; nonattending = less than once a month or not at all. Bold type indicates significant differences for attending and nonattending individuals within a 95 percent confidence interval. General public is native-born.

Putnam argues that both kinds of social capital are important for society, but it is only natural for people of similar backgrounds to stick together and limit most of their interaction with people who are similar to themselves. But when social interaction becomes exclusively limited to people of like backgrounds in very diverse societies, Putnam argues that people can become less trusting of one another, potentially leading to a less stable society.[29]

At least in Canada, however, it does not appear that different immigrant religious groups are less likely than the Canadian general public to be friends with people of other ethnicities or linguistic groups.[30] Immigrants in Canada are far more likely than the Canadian general public to be in regular contact with a friend of a different ethnic or language group than their own. At least a quarter of immigrants have regular contact with friends of different ethnicities or language groups than they speak most of the time. By contrast, only about one in ten Canadians in the general public come into contact with a friend from a different ethnic or language group monthly or more often.

But are these differences in the amount of contact immigrants have with people of different ethnic or linguistic backgrounds affected by religion? At least in Canada, religion seems to have only a moderate influence. First, there are no differences in the frequency of contact with people of different ethnicities and languages among Christian immigrants and immigrants belonging to other religions. Although percentages for each religious group vary slightly, they are not significant, especially when other factors like education are taken into account. The only significant difference is for attending Christian immigrants. In this group, Christian attendees are more likely to have different ethnic friends than Christian nonattendees. It appears that regular involvement in a religious group among Christian immigrants could be a bridge to having friends of different backgrounds.

Social integration, however, is more than interactions between individuals. Relationships with people of different backgrounds, both for immigrants and nonimmigrants, may be a good starting point for the integration of immigrants into society, but immigrants can also be active contributors to society, both locally and nationally.

For example, although Fatima never became a lawyer, she still wanted to help women, regardless of their religious background. But when Mohammed and Fatima started their family, it became clear that with a toddler and a second child on the way, along with Mohammed's long hours at the restaurant, going to law school would not be possible. It was a disappointment for her at first, but then she found another way to help abused women in need. Over a period of two years, she managed to put together a list of agencies—legal, social, and medical—willing to help women in trouble. She also managed to receive some funding from the city to operate her nonprofit organization.

As the executive director of her nonprofit, Fatima was more of a networker than a manager. She became well known in the community as she made the presence of her organization known in her local neighborhood. Many of her leadership skills and contacts within the community were drawn from her time as a volunteer in the local Islamic society. While volunteering, she not only got to know her community better but also became more confident in roles of leadership, including public speaking. In some ways, by being an active part of her local religious center, she became an active part of her community and a recognized citizen of

Toulouse. She often had meetings with city officials and leaders of community organizations, none of whom were Muslim.

Religion can offer immigrants many things in their adjustment to a new place. Immigrants involved with immigrant congregations can have better mental health, but religious organizations can also provide immigrants a platform to become leaders in their communities, creating a pathway for social mobility and higher esteem from the general public, and ultimately making them integrated citizens of their cities and countries.[31] Consequently, religion can be a positive force for the social and civic integration of immigrants.

Historically, we can see how this has worked in the United States for Catholic immigrants and their children. With millions of Catholic immigrants arriving over a hundred years ago, parishes and Catholic organizations became a central part of immigrant communities. Not only did parishes provide a place of refuge for immigrants; Catholic immigrants also built a parallel education system whereby immigrants with socioeconomic disadvantages could send their children to Catholic schools. The hope was that these institutions would not only maintain religious loyalty for subsequent generations but also provide mobility for Catholic immigrants.[32]

In addition to these more historical patterns, religion can help immigrants socially integrate in other, more everyday ways. For instance, immigrants do not always have the opportunity to be leaders in their neighborhoods. Many of these roles go to nonimmigrants who know the culture and may speak the language better. But immigrant churches and other religious organizations offer immigrants opportunities for leadership development.[33] By becoming volunteer leaders in local religious organizations, immigrants can hone public-speaking skills, learn how to manage organizations in the new country, and ultimately become community leaders. This leadership development involves learning many valuable skills that are potentially useful for career advancement and for becoming important contributors to society.[34]

To get a sense of how involvement in a religious organization can

Table 3.5. Percentage of New U.S. Immigrants Who Became a
U.S. Citizen or Plan on Becoming a U.S. Citizen

Immigrant religious group	Total	Attending immigrants	Nonattending immigrants
Christian immigrants	81%	82%	81%
Other religion immigrants	76%	**85%**	74%
Religiously unaffiliated immigrants	85%	n/a	n/a

Source: New Immigrant Survey Round 2 (2009).

Note: Attending = monthly or more often; nonattending = less than once a month or not at all. Bold type indicates significant differences for attending and nonattending individuals within a 95 percent confidence interval.

help immigrants become active citizens of society, in 2009 researchers interviewed new immigrants to the United States who were eligible or would soon be eligible for U.S. citizenship. Although the percentage of immigrants who became U.S. citizens or stated they intended to become U.S. citizens slightly varied across different religious groups, the differences are not statistically significant, especially when other factors like country of origin or education are taken into account. All in all, most U.S. immigrants in this survey had become U.S. citizens or were planning on doing so in the near future.

However, religious attendance may have a role in determining who becomes a citizen. A full 85 percent of attending immigrants belonging to non-Christian religions are U.S. citizens or plan on becoming so. By contrast, only 74 percent of nonattending immigrants belonging to other religions are or plan on becoming U.S. citizens. It appears that there is a connection between religious attendance and becoming a U.S. citizen, at least for religious minorities.[35] This seems to fit the paradigm presented earlier: religious attendees have greater opportunities to become active contributors to U.S. society.

Once immigrants become citizens of the new country, they then have the right to vote in national elections. Voting behavior is often used as a proxy for civic involvement, so it is important to see whether there are religious differences among immigrants, both in which religious groups they belong to and in their involvement in religious organizations. In both the United States and Europe, immigrants who are citizens of their country of residence are less likely to vote than nonimmigrants. In the United States, about seven in ten Americans claimed to have voted in the previous national election, but slightly less than half of both Christian and religious-minority immigrants voted in the previous national U.S. election. In Western Europe, about eight in ten Europeans voted in the previous national election while around six in ten Christian and religious-minority immigrants voted.

Within these lower voting rates for immigrants are no religious-affiliation (Christian, other religions) differences. But there are some differences by religious attendance. In both the United States and Europe, members of the general public who attend religious services monthly or more often are significantly more likely to vote than those who attend less often or not at all. Attendance doesn't seem to matter in determining whether Christian immigrants in Europe or the United States vote, but it does for religious minority immigrants in Europe. Immigrants in Europe belonging to non-Christian religions and regularly attending religious services are significantly more likely to vote than those who do not attend religious services regularly. Remaining religious groups in each context vote at equal rates regardless of whether they attend religious services frequently or not.

This higher voting rate among religiously active minority immigrants in Europe may come as a surprise to some Europeans. In a place where

Table 3.6. Percentage of Citizens Who Voted in the Last National Election

Immigrant religious group and religious attendance	United States	Western Europe
General public	71%	81%
Attending, general public	**80%**	**88%**
Nonattending, general public	64%	79%
Attending, Christian immigrants	48%	60%
Nonattending, Christian immigrants	44%	63%
Attending, other religion immigrants	49%	**63%**
Nonattending, other religion immigrants	47%	53%

Sources: U.S.: General Social Survey 2000–2010. Western Europe: European Social Survey 2002–2010.

Note: Attending = monthly or more often; nonattending = less than once a month or not at all. Bold type indicates significant differences for attending and nonattending individuals within a 95 percent confidence interval. Sample is limited to citizens of their country of residence, including immigrants. General public is native-born.

religion is often described as a barrier for immigrant integration, it seems that the metaphor begins to break down when it comes to civic duties like voting. It appears that religiously active immigrants belonging to religious minority groups (mostly Muslim) who are citizens of their new countries are also more active at the voting booth.[36]

Fatima's experience seems to agree with the patterns found in the preceding statistics. Being a volunteer in her local Islamic association (or mosque) prepared her to become a greater contributor to her community and ultimately a more involved citizen. Similarly, religious attendance doesn't hinder immigrants from becoming citizens or from voting in Europe or the United States. In fact, regular religious attendance is associated with higher citizenship rates for religious minority immigrants in the United States and higher voting rates for religious minorities in Europe.

An Integrated Faith or a Faith Integrated?

Immigrant faith is intricately connected to the way immigrants adjust or integrate into their new countries, but the role of religion is dependent on many things, including type of adjustment, whether immigrants belong to the Christian majority or a religious minority, and, lastly, context. In some instances, religion can be a help for immigrant integration; at other times, it can be less helpful.

Religion can be a bridge for immigrant integration in two ways. First, in almost all contexts, immigrants who regularly participate in a religious organization are happier and are less likely to be depressed or experience emotional distress. This seems to be particularly true for religious minorities in Europe and Canada, where some of these immigrants belonging to non-Christian faiths may experience greater challenges in the job market.

Second, immigrant faith can also help immigrants become contributing members of society. Although there are few differences in citizenship acquisition or voting patterns between Christian immigrants and those belonging to other religions, regular religious attendance is associated with higher citizenship rates in the United States for religious minorities and higher voting rates for religious minorities in Europe. Also, religious attendance in Canada seems to bring Christian immigrants into greater contact with people of different ethnic and linguistic backgrounds.

Mohammed and Fatima experienced these bridging patterns of religion first-hand. Mohammed was emotionally comforted when he went to the mosque for prayer. Fatima became an active citizen in her city through her relationships with other mosque attendees. Psychologically and socially speaking, religion helps immigrants integrate into society. In these ways, immigrant faith is an integrated faith.

But there are instances where religion can be a barrier for immigrants or serve to be less helpful in integrating immigrants into society. Most notably, immigrants belonging to religious minorities (mostly Muslim) in Europe, and to a degree in Canada, are less likely to be employed than other immigrants. This pattern seems to coincide with differences in religious context between the United States and Europe whereby immigrants in Europe and to an extent in Canada may be distinguished by religious affiliation (sometimes in negative ways). Regardless of where immigrants live, however, being an active part of a religious organization doesn't seem to help or hinder immigrants in finding a job or in advancing their careers.

Mohammed also felt this lack of economic opportunities because of his faith. Although he managed to become self-employed, he struggled in finding a job, most likely because he was Muslim. In this way, Mohammed's experience illustrates how religion can be less helpful in economically integrating some immigrants in some contexts.

Most of these conclusions about immigrant faith and integration rely on evidence for one point in time. Consequently, it is altogether possible that happiness leads immigrants to be more religious or that being an active citizen leads to higher levels of religious attendance. In these ways, it is challenging to decipher whether faith is the integrating force or whether immigrant integration (or lack thereof) leads to a changing faith. The direction of many of the findings presented in this chapter could theoretically go either way. In reality, it is probably a combination of the two; without more time-related information, it is difficult to be sure. Both processes could occur in an immigrant's life.

It is not until we see what happens with the children of immigrants and the role of religion within their lives that we can more definitively determine both how an immigrant's faith is changing and how religion shapes the integration of immigrants. By doing so, we can more accurately pinpoint whether the patterns of faith and integration in this chapter among first-generation immigrants are part of a broader pattern that carries through to their adult children. For this reason, we turn to the next generation, the adult children of immigrants.

4

Transferring Faith

Chris and Linda are a young, married couple living in the Washington, D.C., area. Having both grown up in Asian American homes, they have a common background of being raised by immigrant parents from Taiwan. With their newborn son, George, Chris and Linda have in many ways achieved the American dream envisioned by their parents. They live in a suburban home, hold well-paying, professional jobs, and are active members of their community.

Also to the approval of their parents, Chris and Linda attend an Asian American church. The church offers Chris and Linda a group of friends that made their initial adjustment to the D.C. area more welcoming. Not only has the church provided a place to meet new people; it has also given them a common group of friends who understand their Asian American background.

But Chris's and Linda's faith stories began much earlier, mostly with their parents. Chris's parents came to the United States to further their education and begin professional careers. After finishing graduate school, Chris's father found a job in Houston. It was also around this time that Chris, the eldest of his siblings, was born. When Chris was a toddler, his parents regularly attended a Chinese church, an activity they had been introduced to while in graduate school. His parents enjoyed the Asian community offered at the church, and became members within a few years.

Soon after, Chris's family moved to Chicago when his father received a job transfer. As they settled into their new city, Chris's parents again joined a Chinese church. It was during these years, that Chris became introduced to faith at an early age. Chris's parents strove to pass on their faith to their son through prayer before meals, regular reading of the Bible, and regular involvement in their church. However, Chris's faith became more real for him as he entered junior high school. Mentored by youth workers in the English ministry of his parents' church, he grew in his spiritual commitment as he found ways to identify with Christianity apart from the cultural traditions associated with his parents' faith. With all these religious influences, Chris decided to become a Christian during his high school years.

Meanwhile, Linda's religious upbringing was much different. Also from Taiwan, Linda's parents came to the United States seeking financial mobility, not education. They opened a small, yet popular, Chinese restaurant in Tennessee, working day and night to make a living for their three daughters. With their busy days, religion was very distant from their minds. They claimed no particular religion as their own, even though they occasionally offered some food sacrifices in memory of their ancestors and prayed from time to time.

Linda's parents wanted more opportunities for their children than they had experienced in the United States. Since Linda's parents thought the public schools in their area would not adequately prepare their children for university, they sent all three of their children to private school. The best private school in their area was an evangelical Christian school. Linda's parents knew about the religious nature of the school, but were not concerned by it. For them, the potential educational success for their children was more important than the school's religious teaching.

Needless to say, Linda grew up with a strained spiritual life. At home, she would see her parents and live-in grandmother practice religious traditions from Taiwan. At school, she learned about the Bible and devotion to Jesus. Adding to this tension, growing up Asian American in the U.S. South was extremely challenging for Linda. She had few friends and rarely saw her parents due to their work responsibilities.

Her religious life became suddenly real when she and her family were taken hostage in a home invasion. As the hostage takers threatened her family's lives, she prayed to Jesus for help, promising to serve him if she and her family were saved. Fortunately, Linda's family survived and was not physically harmed. From then on, Linda sought to understand the teachings of Jesus better. There were ups and downs to her spiritual pilgrimage, but she always came back to the three things taught to her in the Christian school: go to church, read the Bible, and never stop praying.

Both Chris and Linda were encouraged by their parents to pursue higher education. For Chris, youth workers in his church also strongly encouraged university. For Linda, her private, Christian school was instrumental in preparing her for college. Upon graduating high school, Chris and Linda both enrolled in top universities in their states. Chris pursued a degree in engineering while Linda took a degree in economics, followed by a graduate degree in public health.

Following college, Chris got a government job in northern Virginia. Linda did contract work with various think tanks and policy centers in Washington, D.C. Now living in the same city, Chris and Linda met each other for the first time at Grace Church, begun in 2001 by a small group of second-generation Asian Americans. The church's mission was to provide a place where Asian American professionals could gather for worship and community in the Washington, D.C., area. Chris started going to the church because it offered him a way to connect to spiritual things with people his own age while still maintaining his Asian heritage. Linda checked out the church upon a recommendation of a friend and liked the weekly Bible studies offered near her apartment building.

Chris and Linda eventually dated, got engaged, and became husband and wife. And Chris and Linda's parents couldn't be more proud of them. They landed good jobs after college and graduate school, they are homeowners, and they have a healthy, busy boy. For their parents, the parental, financial, and *spiritual* investments they made in Chris and Linda are paying off.

Does Immigrant Faith Get Transferred?

After preparing for the journey to a new country, adjusting to life in a new place, and eventually becoming long-term residents, immigrants undergo substantial changes in their lives. In light of this sea of change, immigrant parents are often eager to instill religious values and traditions within their children. Given the cultural challenges many immigrants face in a new country, immigrants often want their adult children to carry on their cultural heritage. This can mean continuing ethnic traditions or speaking the parents' language. At the same time, many immigrants will also look to their ethno-religious community as a means to pass on their cultural roots.[1]

Despite the best intentions of immigrants, the forces of adaptation to the destination country are sometimes greater than the cultural influences found in the immigrant home.

Immigration scholars have shown how adult children of immigrants (or the second generation) are more like their peers with no migration background than like their parents' generation.[2] And although each subsequent generation may return to some traditions of previous generations, later generations typically become more and more like the mainstream culture surrounding them.[3] These types of changes occur at all levels of life, including language, health, political activity, educational attainment, and economic status. Second-generation immigrants speak the national language of their country of residence, are engaged in politics, often become more highly educated than their parents, and in many instances have a higher economic status than first-generation immigrants.[4]

But do adult children of immigrants also religiously adapt? On the surface, the answer is not altogether clear. As mentioned earlier, Will Herberg, a prominent sociologist during the middle of the twentieth century, proposed that first-generation immigrants in the United States would cling close to religion. But, he also predicted that religion would be of less importance for the second generation. This lack of religious identity for the children of immigrants could be considered adaptation compared with the ethnic religion practiced by their parents' generation. But recent studies have found things to be more complicated than this linear decrease of religion among children of immigrants. Apparently, things don't move along in such a straight-line fashion for all religious groups. Interruptions occur, often dependent on factors like the ethnic background of the second generation, the involvement of parents, and the community in which immigrant children are raised.[5]

For example, Chris and Linda may have ended up in the same faith community in Washington, D.C., but their spiritual paths were very different. Chris inherited the faith of his parents, something that was very important to them. His parents had become convinced of a new religious paradigm while living in the United States. They did not want Chris to abandon their new-found faith by either reverting back to traditional ancestor worship or simply having no faith at all. By contrast, Linda grew into her faith as she witnessed religion being played out in real events in her life. Although her faith was not exactly passed down to her by her parents, her family did lead her indirectly toward Christianity by sending her to a Christian school.

Therefore, one way to evaluate whether an immigrant's faith is transferred is to measure religious change from the immigrant generation to the second generation. As discussed in chapter 2, religious switching from one religious group to another is not that common among immigrants. For the most part, immigrants remain in the same religious group they were raised in even if they completely change religious contexts. If any religious change occurs, it mostly happens prior to, not after, migration.

But when we look at adult children of immigrants, religious switching is more common. In the United States, for example, only about three-fourths of immigrant children raised in Protestant, Catholic, or "other religion" (Islam, Hinduism, Buddhism) homes today belong to the same religious group. Religious switching is even more common among children of immigrants raised with no religion. Fewer than two-thirds of immigrant children raised in homes with no particular religion still claim no religious affiliation.

Table 4.1. Adult Children of Immigrants' Religious Affiliation in the United States

	Religion raised			
Religion today	Protestant	Catholic	Other religion	No religion
Protestant	**76%**	13%	8%	29%
Catholic	3%	**75%**	1%	5%
Other religion	4%	1%	**73%**	6%
No religion	16%	10%	10%	**60%**
Total	100%	100%	100%	100%

Source: U.S.: General Social Survey 2000–2010.

Note: Bold type indicates retention rates.

Which religions do these religious switchers practice? Many have no religion. Among adult children of immigrants raised in a Protestant religious group, nearly two in ten have no religious affiliation now. About one in ten children of immigrants raised Catholic also has no religion. A similar share of immigrant children raised in other religions also has no religious affiliation.

The other direction religious switchers go is toward Christianity, and more specifically to Protestant groups. More than one in ten immigrant children raised Catholic (about the same ratio of Catholics who switch to no religion) switch to Protestantism, and almost three in ten immigrant children raised with no religion now belong to Protestant groups. This direction of religious switching of immigrant children in the United States is similar to the experience of first-generation immigrants. Certainly the level of switching is much higher among children of immigrants compared with their parents' generation, but the movement often goes to the same two groups: Protestants or no religion.

Chris's and Linda's faith stories agree with patterns of religious change from first to second generations. Like Chris, a large share of second-generation immigrants raised in a Protestant religion remains in that religion. As with Linda, one of the religious groups nonreligious children of immigrants switch to is Protestantism.

And for trends among Asian Americans more specifically, Linda's and Chris's experiences are quite ordinary. Further analysis reveals similar patterns for second-generation Asian immigrants as those occurring for all children of immigrants. About two-thirds of Asian American children of immigrants raised Protestant, Catholic, or with no religion are still part of these religious (or nonreligious) groups. Asian American children of immigrants raised Buddhist are even less likely to be Buddhist today with only about half claiming Buddhism as their current religion. By contrast, the highest retention rate of children of immigrants is among other religions (Islam, Hinduism, and others). Nearly three-fourths of Asian American children of immigrants raised in these other religions continue to subscribe to the same religion today.

As is the case with all children of immigrants in the United States, the two religious (or nonreligious) groups benefiting from religious switching among Asian children of immigrants are Protestants and the religious "nones."[6] So Chris's and Linda's experiences are quite representative of those of other Asian children of immigrants living in the United States. Following Chris's experience, not only is the retention rate for Protestants reasonably high, but also a large share of Asian American children of immigrants raised with no religion (like Linda) is now part of a Protestant group.

In many ways, the movement in and out of the Protestant and no-religious-affiliation groups in the United States is evidence for religious adaptation among children of immigrants. Although the United States

Table 4.2. *Asian American Adult Children of Immigrants' Religious Affiliation in the United States*

Religion today	Religion raised				
	Protestant	Catholic	Buddhist	Other religion	No religion
Protestant	**66%**	16%	2%	3%	24%
Catholic	1%	**59%**	0%	3%	6%
Buddhist	2%	0%	**52%**	0%	7%
Other religion	3%	3%	0%	**71%**	5%
No religion	28%	22%	39%	5%	**56%**
Total	100%	100%	100%	100%	100%

Source: Pew Research Center's Asian American Survey 2012.

Note: Bold type indicates retention rates.

was historically founded by Protestants and various brands of Protestantism formed the majority religious group among Americans for hundreds
of years, the number of Americans with no religious affiliation has grown
recently, particularly among younger generations. Therefore, it should
not be surprising that the two groups gaining the greatest number of
religious switchers among adult children of immigrants in the United
States are Protestants and those with no religious affiliation.

Americans are known for fluid religious identities.[7] Many Americans
grow up with one religion, switch to a different one in adulthood, and
sometimes switch several times more before their death. As children of
immigrants switch from one religion to another, they may simply be
adapting to a dynamic religious society rather than adapting to dominant
religious groups.

But religious switching is not limited to children of immigrants in
the United States. Evidence from outside of the United States points to
a similar pattern of religious switching toward religious majorities or
growing religious groups. For example, only about one in ten immigrant
children raised Muslim or in other minority religious groups (besides
Buddhists) in France has left the religion of his or her parents, and a
large percentage of Christian children of immigrants (more than two in
ten) is no longer practicing Christianity. An even greater share (more
than four in ten) of children of immigrants raised in Buddhist homes is
no longer Buddhist. Many children of immigrants raised in Christianity
or Buddhism are opting for no religious affiliation. Although France has
a Catholic heritage, it prides itself on being a secular society; therefore,
it should come as no surprise that the religious "nones" are the prominent recipients of religious switchers among children of immigrants. (As
further evidence of this adaptation to dominant religious groups in the
country, only a small percentage of children of immigrants raised with
no religion now claims a religious affiliation.)

But the France data also reveal a pattern among Muslim immigrants.
An extremely small share of Muslim-raised children of immigrants has
switched to a different religious group. This high retention of Muslim

Table 4.3. Children of Immigrants' Religious Affiliation in France

Religion today	Religion raised				
	Christian	Muslim	Buddhist	Other religion	No religion
Christian	**78%**	0%	1%	0%	4%
Muslim	0%	**89%**	4%	0%	2%
Buddhist	0%	0%	**57%**	0%	0%
Other religion	0%	0%	0%	**90%**	1%
No religion	20%	10%	38%	10%	**93%**
Total	100%	100%	100%	100%	100%

Source: Trajectoires et Origines Survey 2007.

Note: Bold type indicates retention rates.

immigrant children within Islam may indicate a strong religious identity among first- *and* second-generation Muslims, perhaps due to a heightened religious identity in the face of public opposition to Islam. If so, this lack of religious adaptation may be similar to the pattern found among highly religious Muslim immigrants living in areas where anti-immigrant sentiment is also the highest.

In all contexts, the children of immigrants largely stay with their parents' religion; therefore, the transfer of faith is largely successful. Nevertheless, the movement in and out of religious groups among the second generation is much higher than it is among immigrants. In this way, the transfer of faith from one generation to the next is not as smooth as it was for immigrants after moving to a new country. Many children of immigrants switch to religions that are common in their environment. However, this rising similarity of religion with the general public is not always the case for all groups in all contexts. In particular, Muslim immigrants in France, and possibly in the rest of Europe, transfer their faith well into the second generation, with only a small share switching to no religious affiliation when they become adults.

Are Religious Practices Transferred?

Changing one's religion is only one way to measure the transfer of faith from parent to child. Changing involvement in religious organizations is another. If children of immigrants are attending about as frequently as the general public, or if their religious attendance is more similar to that of the general public than the first generation's attendance, such patterns would further confirm a process of religious adaptation rather than a total transfer of faith.

For example, Linda's parents didn't attend religious services when she was a child. But, as Linda better understood her community and the importance American society places on attending religious services, she became far more active in religious groups compared with her parents. By going from nearly no involvement in religious organizations as a child living in an immigrant family to regular activity in a religious group as an adult, Linda was adapting to a religiously active American society.

Nearly half of the U.S. general public attends religious services monthly or more frequently. A higher percentage of Christian immigrants regularly attends religious services, but Christian children of immigrants are more similar to the U.S. general public: about half attend religious services monthly or more often. By contrast, only about a quarter of immigrant children belonging to other religions attend religious services. This is much lower than in the U.S. general public; however, immigrant children belonging to other religions are a uniquely young adult population. Thus, the share of children of immigrants belonging to non-Christian religions is not that different from that of the U.S. general public of similar-aged young adults. In sum, both broad religious

Table 4.4. Percentage Attending Religious Services Monthly or More

Immigrant / children of immigrant religious attendance by religious group	United States	Canada	Western Europe
General public	46%	32%	22%
Christian immigrants	59%	58%	44%
Christian children of immigrants	**52%**	**46%**	**34%**
Other religion immigrants	45%	51%	42%
Other religion children of immigrants	**26%**	49%	40%

Sources: U.S.: General Social Survey 2000–2010. Canada: Ethnic Diversity Survey 2003. Western Europe: European Social Survey 2002–2010.

Note: Bold type indicates significant differences between immigrants and children of immigrants (by religious group) within a 95 percent confidence interval. General public has no migration background.

groups—Christian and non-Christian—are adapting to the religious attendance levels found in the U.S. general public.

Christian children of immigrants in Canada seem to exhibit a similar pattern of religious change as is found among children of immigrants in the United States. In 2003, about one-third of Canadians attended religious services monthly or more often (a much smaller share than in the United States). A much higher percentage of Christian immigrants and immigrants belonging to other faiths regularly attends religious services compared with the Canadian general public. But the percentage gap between Christian children of immigrants and average Canadians regularly attending religious services is smaller.

The share of Christian children of immigrants attending religious services is similar to that of the Canadian general public, but the percentage of non-Christian faiths regularly attending religious services in Canada remains largely unchanged between first and second generations: about half of both immigrants and children of immigrants belonging to non-Christian religions attend religious services monthly or more often. Religious adaptation toward the Canadian general public among children of immigrants seems to occur more among Christians, but less so for other religions.

In Europe, generational change in religious attendance is similar to the Canadian experience. The share of Christian children of immigrants attending religious services is less than that of Christian immigrants and is more in line with the European general public. But, about the same percentage of immigrant children belonging to non-Christian religions attend religious services as first-generation immigrants belonging to the same religious groups.[8]

In all three contexts, the share of children of immigrants attending religious services is lower than that of their parents' generation. This may not be altogether pleasing for immigrant parents who may be trying to transfer their faith into the next generation. Instead, many adult children of immigrants are adapting to the religious environment around them, attending religious services with about the same frequency as the general public. This pattern of adaptation is particularly true for Christian children of immigrants who in all three contexts have similar shares of their group attending religious services as the general public.

However, faith is transferred for religious minorities in Canada and Europe. In both contexts, about the same share of second-generation and first-generation immigrants belonging to non-Christian religions regularly attends religious services. Although it cannot be proven how this stability of faith occurs between religious-minority generations, this pattern of religious resilience in religious attendance is similar to the strong transfer of faith occurring among the same groups when one looks at religious affiliation. As asserted, then, these adult children of immigrants may be responding to a threatened religious identity as they live in a context where their religious-minority position can be a barrier for integrating into society. Other reasons could include strong socialization by their families or perhaps fewer opportunities for religious-minority children of immigrants to interact with youth belonging to different religions.[9] Whatever the underlying causes, religious minorities (and more specifically Muslims) in Europe are not becoming less religious from one generation to the next in contexts where religion can be a barrier for the adjustment of immigrants belonging to non-Christian groups.

Are Faith and Integration Patterns Transferred?

In chapter 3, religion was found to influence immigrant adjustment. On the one hand, religious attendance helped ease some of the psychological troubles immigrants experienced, especially for religious minorities in contexts where religion was more of a barrier to their adjustment. Involvement in a religious group was also correlated with higher citizenship and voting rates. On the other hand, religion was a hindrance for some religious groups in some places. For example, immigrant religious minorities in Europe (and to a degree in Canada) are less likely to be employed than the general public. But are these patterns transferred into the second generation? Does religion provide the same benefits or challenges to the socioeconomic integration of second-generation immigrants as it did for their first-generation parents?

Education

One of the main advantages second-generation immigrants have over their parents' generation is greater access to education. This is particularly true for postsecondary education or years of education beyond high school. Several studies across the United States, Canada, and Western Europe show how children of immigrants often have more schooling than their parents' generation.[10] Although the generational increase varies across different origin and ethnic groups, the general direction in educational attainment for most immigrant groups is in an upward one. But how does educational attainment differ across religious groups?

Children of immigrants of both Christian and other religious backgrounds seem to have levels of education fairly equal to those in the general public in each context. Although things may be different for specific religious groups in specific European countries, the general pattern is that no one religious group is less or more likely to have some college education than the general public.[11] This is especially true after the socioeconomic background of parents is taken into account.

Table 4.5. Percentage with Some College Education

Children of immigrants' religious group and religious attendance	United States	Canada	Western Europe
General public	62%	77%	36%
Attending, general public	**68%**	**80%**	36%
Nonattending, general public	57%	76%	36%
Attending, Christian children of immigrants	**73%**	**88%**	**54%**
Nonattending, Christian children of immigrants	50%	81%	40%
Attending, other religion children of immigrants	n/a	93%	30%
Nonattending, other religion children of immigrants	n/a	89%	38%

Sources: U.S.: General Social Survey 2000–2010. Canada: Canada General Social Survey 2004, 2006, 2008, 2009. Western Europe: European Social Survey 2002–2010.

Note: Bold type indicates significant differences for attending and nonattending individuals within a 95 percent confidence interval. Samples limited to respondents aged 25–44. General public has no migration background.

However, both statistical studies and interviews with second-generation immigrants in the United States indicate that involvement in a religious group helps them achieve even greater educational opportunities.[12] In essence, a strong community of faith can become an important support group in encouraging children of immigrants toward and preparing them for educational success. Consequently, religious attendance, rather than religious affiliation, may make more of a difference in the educational success of children of immigrants.

For example, Chris and Linda both received strong encouragement from their parents to succeed academically. Both were raised in homes where homework was completed well and on time. Their parents expected high exam grades and would sometimes give their children additional homework for extra practice. Although religion didn't seem to matter much in Chris's and Linda's parents' motivation for their children's academic success (remember that Chris's family was Christian and Linda's family had no particular religion), each of their religious situations only further encouraged academic success. Chris's peer reference group at church also strongly encouraged good grades, as did the youth workers who spiritually mentored Chris. Linda's school regularly equated good grades with a good, Christian lifestyle. In both instances, religious activity went hand in hand with high academic goals.

By a large margin, Christian children of immigrants in the United States who regularly attend religious services are more likely to have some college education compared with Christian children of immigrants who rarely or never attend religious services. Almost three-quarters of Christian children of immigrants in the United States attending religious services have some college education, while only half of attendees have a similar amount of education. A similar bump in education, albeit not as large, exists for Christian children of immigrants in Canada and also in Europe.

Religious attendance was a help for immigrants in societies like the United States and Canada where religious organizations have an important civic role within society. This pattern of religion as a bridge for integration into society is transferred to Christian second-generation immigrants in these contexts. Additionally, religious attendance also has an impact on second-generation education for Christians in Europe.

However, the religious-attendance premium for education doesn't seem to occur for other, non-Christian religious groups. Adult children of immigrants belonging to religious-minority groups and regularly attending religious services are not any more likely in Canada or Europe to have some college education compared with those attending less frequently. In this way, there is also a transfer of faith from immigrant to child since religious attendance had little impact on socioeconomic integration for religious-minority immigrants.[13]

Employment

Although religious attendance seems to make a difference in the educational success of Christian children of immigrants in the United States, Canada, and Europe, it is a much less important factor in finding a job. Only among attending Christian children of immigrants in Europe do attendees have significantly higher employment rates. But, even within this group, the actual difference in employment rates is not that large.

The crucial religious difference in employment is not attendance but religious affiliation, particularly in Europe. Both attending and

Table 4.6. Percentage Employed

Children of immigrants' religious group and religious attendance	United States	Canada	Western Europe
General public	94%	98%	94%
Attending, general public	95%	98%	94%
Nonattending, general public	94%	97%	94%
Attending, Christian children of immigrants	95%	97%	**98%**
Nonattending, Christian children of immigrants	92%	97%	92%
Attending, other religion children of immigrants	n/a	96%	90%
Nonattending, other religion children of immigrants	n/a	97%	84%

Sources: U.S.: General Social Survey 2000–2010. Canada: Canada General Social Survey 2004, 2006, 2008, 2009. Western Europe: European Social Survey 2002–2010.

Note: Bold type indicates significant differences for attending and nonattending individuals within a 95 percent confidence interval. Samples limited to respondents aged 25–44. General public has no migration background.

nonattending children of immigrants belonging to other religions in Europe (mostly Muslim) are significantly less likely to be employed than the European general public. This lower employment among religious-minority children of immigrants in Europe is similar to the low levels of employment for first-generation religious minorities. By contrast, Christian children of immigrants in Europe have employment levels equal to those in the general public, and children of immigrants in both Christian and other religious groups in the United States and Canada are as likely to have a job as the general public in these countries.

The same religious employment barrier resulting from being a religious minority in Europe, or more specifically a Muslim, is transferred into the second generation, even when other factors like education and the socioeconomic status of parents is taken into account. Further analysis finds that second-generation Muslims are still less likely to be employed even when differences in religiosity, personal values, and ethnicity between the general public and second-generation Muslims in Europe are accounted for.[14] Although Muslim unemployment in the second generation may be more prominent in some European countries than others, additional research has demonstrated that second-generation Muslims are less likely to be employed in the UK, France, and Germany, even when other factors are held constant.

Occupation

However, once children of immigrants are in a job, how does religion help or hinder them as they strive for better careers? Do the bridging (in the United States and to an extent in Canada) and barrier (in Europe and to an extent in Canada) patterns of religion found in first-generation immigrants carry through into their occupational mobility as well?

It seems they do again, for some religious groups, in some places. Following the pattern of religious bridges in the United States and Canada, Christian children of immigrants regularly attending religious services are significantly more likely to be in a professional occupation than their

Table 4.7. Percentage Working in a Professional Occupation

Children of immigrants' religious group and religious attendance	United States	Canada	Western Europe
General public	49%	50%	47%
Attending, general public	**53%**	**55%**	**48%**
Nonattending, general public	45%	50%	46%
Attending, Christian children of immigrants	**60%**	**61%**	60%
Nonattending, Christian children of immigrants	37%	52%	55%
Attending, other religion children of immigrants	n/a	**78%**	51%
Nonattending, other religion children of immigrants	n/a	63%	55%

Sources: U.S.: General Social Survey 2000–2010. Canada: Canada General Social Survey 2004, 2006, 2008, 2009. Western Europe: European Social Survey 2002–2010.

Note: Bold type indicates significant differences for attending and nonattending individuals within a 95 percent confidence interval. Samples limited to employed respondents aged 25–44. General public has no migration background.

nonattending counterparts. As expected, the occupational mobility of children of immigrants seems to be positively associated with active involvement in a local church in places where religious attendance is high (like the United States, and to an extent in Canada). Interestingly, in Canada, this is even the case for religious minorities.[15]

Chris and Linda's church in Washington, D.C., serves as a tangible example of how religious involvement in a Christian group can help occupational success. Chris and Linda's church consists of people who are similar in many ways. Not only do most have an Asian background, but most also work in professional jobs. Sermons on Sundays and Bible teaching in small groups throughout the week encourage church members to give their all to their careers, not for the sake of personal advancement, but as testimony to the presence of Jesus in their lives. This environment may not have initially landed Chris and Linda occupational success, but it has certainly been a factor in their retaining their current occupations. Surrounded by a highly professional group of people in their church, regular attendees like Chris and Linda are offered a peer support group that helps them advance in their careers. In these ways, religious attendance is a natural bridge to their occupational success.

But how about the religious-minority barrier seen earlier for second-generation employment in Europe? Compared with the European general public, children of immigrants belonging to other religions have no significantly different occupational status. Similarly, Christian children of immigrants are as likely to have a professional job as the European general public. And given the rather secular nature of Europe and its low religious attendance, there seem to be no differences in the occupational statuses of attending or nonattending children of immigrants. The religious barrier seen in employment among religious minorities in Europe does not apply to occupational attainment once second-generation immigrants belonging to non-Christian religions find a job. In this way, the religious barrier connected with a lower chance of being in a professional occupation for religious-minority, first-generation immigrants in Europe is not transferred into the next generation.

Voting

Beyond economics, religion can also be a help or hindrance for the social incorporation of children of immigrants. A variety of measures such as feelings of belonging, trust in society, social interactions with people of various backgrounds, and choice of residential location (predominantly immigrant or predominantly nonimmigrant neighborhoods) are used to show whether children of immigrants are becoming full members of society. Another important measure is their participation in democracy as indicated by voting. As found among immigrants in chapter 3, religion does have a bearing on voting rates. More specifically, religious minority immigrants in Europe were more likely to vote when they attended religious services.

However, religious attendance for second-generation immigrants is more of a benefit for Christians, not religious minority groups. Christian children of immigrants in the United States and Europe are more likely to vote when they are regularly attending religious services. This same premium of religious attendance on voting does not occur among second-generation religious minorities in Europe. In fact, second-generation religious minorities are significantly less likely to vote than the general

Table 4.8. Percentage of Citizens Who Voted in Last National Election

Children of immigrants' religious group and religious attendance	United States	Western Europe
General public	71%	81%
Attending, general public	**80%**	**88%**
Nonattending, general public	64%	79%
Attending, Christian children of immigrants	**84%**	81%
Nonattending, Christian children of immigrants	61%	80%
Attending, other religion children of immigrants	n/a	59%
Nonattending, other religion children of immigrants	n/a	58%

Sources: U.S.: General Social Survey 2000–2010. Western Europe: European Social Survey 2002–2010.

Note: Bold type indicates significant differences for attending and nonattending individuals within a 95 percent confidence interval. General public has no migration background.

public. In Europe, about eight in ten citizens voted in a previous national election while fewer than six in ten children of immigrants belonging to minority religions voted. The explanation for this is not clear, but it may be a result of the assertion expressed earlier that religion is a barrier among religious minorities in Europe. Second-generation religious minorities may feel disenfranchised by European society, their religious values may not encourage active participation in democracy, or perhaps they represent a more youthful population that is less likely to vote in the first place. But even when these factors are considered, second-generation religious minorities in Europe (mostly Muslims) are still less likely to vote than the European general public.

All in all, many of the religious patterns found among immigrants and their integration into society are transferred to adult children of immigrants. Involvement in a religious group is associated with higher educational and occupational levels, particularly for Christians in the United States and to an extent in Canada. This helping effect of religious attendance on the economic status of Christian children of immigrants fits religion's role as a bridge in societies where religious attendance is relatively high and an important part of civic life.

By contrast, the religious barriers experienced by immigrant religious minorities in Europe seem to also transfer into the next generation. Although children of immigrants belonging to religious minorities are not any less likely to work in a professional job compared with the European general public, children of immigrants belonging to religious minority groups in Europe (mostly Muslim) are significantly less likely to have a job in the first place. Also, children of immigrants belonging to non-Christian religions are less likely to vote.

A Faith Transferred or a Transferred Faith?

Immigrants who value their religious heritage look for ways to transfer their faith beyond their own generation. They may not expect their children to practice their religion exactly the same way as they did in the origin country, but many immigrants hold the expectation that their adult children will continue to actively identify with their religion and pass it down to their own children.

However, the statistical evidence does not indicate that the immigrant's faith is altogether transferred to all children of immigrants. Some children of immigrants switch religions from the ones in which they were raised. In the United States, this means that some children of immigrants with no religious affiliation join Protestant groups while some Protestants and Catholics opt for no religious affiliation. In Europe, many children of immigrants raised in Christian homes claim no religious affiliation once they become adults. Moreover, even the intensity of faith as measured by attendance at religious services changes from one generation to the next. Christian children of immigrants in all contexts attend religious services less frequently than immigrants. All this intergenerational religious change seems to indicate a religious adaptation to nonmigrant peers. In these ways, the immigrant's faith is not completely transferred to the next generation.

Chris and Linda understand what it is like to see their faith transferred and at times not transferred from their parents to themselves. Chris has mostly followed his parents' Christian faith, albeit the manner and frequency with which he practices it are more like those of his peer, American-born group than like his parents' set of traditions. Linda is not practicing the faith (or lack thereof) of her family. Through different life experiences, she was drawn to Christianity, following a way of life shown to her in her Christian school. As the statistics bear out, sometimes, as in Chris's experience, faith is transferred; at other times, as in Linda's experience, it is not.

However, religious change is not the whole story. Faith can be transferred in other ways, including patterns in the way religion shapes the socioeconomic integration of second-generation immigrants. At times, religious attendance can have some positive influences on adult children of immigrants, namely, in the higher education and occupational attainment of Christian children of immigrants in the United States and to an extent in Canada. And in the United States, religious attendance seems to be associated with a higher likelihood of becoming a full citizen of society as indicated by a higher incidence of voting. So although the faith of children of immigrants may be somewhat different from their parents' faith, religion can still provide a helpful avenue for socioeconomic success among some children of immigrants, particularly for Christians in places like the United States and Canada, where religious activity is an important part of everyday life. The immigrant's faith may not always be transferred in Christian children of immigrants, but for those who have remained active in a Christian faith, it can be a dynamic faith that helps children of immigrants expand their quality of life vis-à-vis their parents' generation.

Chris sticking with the Christian faith taught to him by his parents and Linda becoming a Christian have certainly opened up opportunities for their socioeconomic success that might have not otherwise been available to them. While growing up, their Christian peers and leaders strongly encouraged academic success, including university attendance. This led to Chris and Linda working in professional jobs. Even today, continued participation in their Christian church provides a supportive environment in helping Chris and Linda be all they can be in their jobs, leading to even greater occupational success.

However, some of the religious patterns seen among religious-minority immigrants in Europe, and somewhat in Canada, continue into the next generation. In this way, immigrants transfer the socioeconomic patterns associated with faith to their adult children. Immigrants belonging to religious minorities (mostly Muslims) in Europe rarely change religious groups and they also attend religious services about as often as their parents' generation. And although religious attendance doesn't result in huge differences in their socioeconomic status, simply belonging to a religious minority is associated with lower employment for adult children of immigrants in Europe. This pattern of lower employment among Muslim children of immigrants in Europe is a continuation of a similar trend seen among first-generation Muslim immigrants. In this way, faith, although perhaps in a less helpful sense, is transferred from one generation to another.

In some instances, the immigrant's faith is transferred. In other cases, it is not. However, the transferring of faith is only one part of the story of important patterns of faith across immigrant generations. It seems that more limited religious patterns among first-generation immigrants can become more established trends for the next generation. This indicates the presence of some common themes of religious change and integration for immigrants and their adult children throughout the United States, Canada, and Western Europe. It is to these common themes that we now turn to in the conclusion as the various components of immigrant faith—a moving, changing, integrating, and transferring faith—are woven together.

Conclusion

Weaving Immigrant Faith Together

The stories of immigrant faith are as many as the millions of migrants who have moved from one country to another. For Guo Kai Li in Montreal or Mohammed and Fatima in Toulouse or Chris and Linda in Washington, D.C., religion was important for at least parts of their story. For others, like Pedro and Lucinda in New Jersey or Zhang Yi in Montreal, faith was more of a side issue. Whatever the story, it cannot be denied that religion, or the absence of religion, was consequential to the way these immigrants lived their new lives in their new countries.

The immigrant stories presented throughout this book were based on real people and events. Stories such as these often remain hidden from public view and are only known by those who are intimately connected with immigrant communities. As presented in the introduction, examples of immigrant faith also appear in our newspapers and on our television screens. Sometimes these reports crop up because of legal issues. For example, the story of Gunbar Singh Multani in Montreal illustrates how immigrant religious practices such as carrying symbols of faith can come into conflict with laws in the new country. Sometimes religion is used by immigrants to help them sort out legal issues, such as when many of the members of the Buen Pastor congregation in North Carolina were facing deportation. At other times, the public story is about grievances, protests, and sometimes violence, such as the riots of Muslim youth in France. Finally, the back story of fame, as in the case of Jeremy Lin, is sometimes interwoven with a story of immigrant faith.

However, these stories in the public's conversation are not always well understood. Without a deeper knowledge of patterns in immigrant faith, it is not always possible to know the *complete* story. The analogy of a woven tapestry bears repeating. Individual stories of immigrant faith represent only several strands of thread that form part of a much larger piece. When they are seen independently of each other, it is difficult to understand how one immigrant's story is part of broader patterns of immigrant faith. But when the various stories are woven together into a single tapestry, we can see the broader patterns and how the faith of immigrants is moved, changed, integrated, and transferred. Quantitative data, like that presented in this book, represent the voices of thousands of immigrants. Such data assist us in uncovering these patterns of immigrant faith.

This book's purpose has been to contextualize broad patterns of immigrant religious adaptation within the stories of immigrants. The chapters were presented in a fairly chronological order, starting with the act of migration, followed by changes in immigrant faith, religion's role in shaping immigrant adjustment, and, finally, the role of faith for children of immigrants. However, this sequential ordering of events can disguise some overarching themes occurring throughout the immigrant's life. Using the tapestry metaphor again, sometimes patterns can be seen from different vantage points. One pattern is clearly visible when one looks at the tapestry one way, but once the tapestry is turned around, another set of patterns can be seen. This conclusion attempts to do just this, recapping the patterns presented in each chapter but reordering them in a different way so that patterns occurring across the chapters can be better understood.

Religious Identity versus Religious Practice

Two key religion variables are presented throughout this book: religious identity (religious affiliation with a particular religious group) and religious practice (frequency of religious attendance at religious services).

Although there are many ways to measure both religious identity and religious practice, these are the most common variables available in statistical data of immigrants and the general public. Despite some shortcomings in the way these variables measure religious identity and practice, they are still useful in describing some aspects of immigrant faith, from migration through to the role of religion for the second generation. Sometimes religious identity is influential for some stage of an immigrant's experience. At other times it is only religious practice that is important. In other instances, both matter. And in some cases, neither religious affiliation nor religious attendance is important.

Some religious groups (or religious identities) are more likely to move than others. It seems that religious minorities in the origin country are more likely to move, often moving to countries where their religion is the majority religion. For example, not all immigrants from Latin America to the United States are Catholic. Although Catholicism has a long history in Latin America, the number of Protestants and those with no religious affiliation has been growing. Also, there is evidence that Protestants, perhaps because of church connections in a largely Protestant United States, are more likely to migrate than Catholic counterparts. The Buen Pastor church in North Carolina is an example. In many ways, this church's theological and religious convictions are in line with a deeply religious, Protestant, southern United States. The members of Buen Pastor church may be foreigners, but that does not mean that they brought a foreign religion. By contrast, religious practice or differing levels of religiosity seem to play a less influential role in migration. Although immigrants crossing treacherous border situations or wading through bureaucratic red tape may use their faith for emotional support, it does not appear that religious practice has a huge bearing on who leaves a country or who stays.

After migration, an immigrant's faith changes, but not in the same way for both his or her religious identity and his or her religious practice. Although some immigrants may switch in and out of various Christian denominations or move from or into no religious affiliation, most immigrants maintain their religious identity after migration. In some contexts, especially where their religion is markedly different from the majority religion in the new country, their religious identity could become even more important than before they moved. For example, the Multani household in Montreal felt they needed to defend their religious identity in Canada. Since Sikhs are a religious minority in both India and Canada, maintaining that faith was important, even if it meant dealing with challenging legal issues.

However, statistics show that immigrants do, over time, adapt their religious practices to become more like the general public around them. Not only do religious organizations start to look more like religious institutions in the general public; religious attendance levels of immigrants start to mirror the religious attendance levels of the general public in their local areas. (This religious adaptation occurs after a short-term drop in overall religious attendance immediately following migration, presumably due to the pressures of entering a new place with many things to learn, including the religious context.) Although religious identities are slow to change for immigrants, religious practices can significantly change as they adjust to their new lives in the new country.

On the one hand, religious identity can also shape immigrant economic success. For example, it appears that immigrant religious minorities are less likely to be employed and less likely to hold professional jobs when living in contexts where religion has a relatively close relationship with the state and religious minorities represent a large share of the destination country's immigrants. For example, some have argued that the high level of underemployment among Muslims in France was a driving factor leading to the weeks of riots in 2005.

On the other hand, religious attendance is a potential bridge for immigrant integration. In some instances, immigrants who regularly attend religious services are more likely to become new citizens and eventually vote in national elections. Also, most immigrants attending religious services are happier than those who do not regularly attend religious services. For instance, although the members of Buen Pastor church experienced significant legal difficulties, they were able to understand their predicament through a spiritual lens, giving many of their members a feeling of peace about the situation.

Lastly, religious identity and practice can influence the lives of children of immigrants. For many, religious affiliation and attendance become more like their peer group's than their parents'. For some immigrant religious groups, there is a decline in immigrant children identifying with the same religion as their parents, particularly for Christian groups like Catholics and Protestants, as well as some non-Christian groups like Buddhists. Many of these immigrant children switch to having no religious affiliation or change their religion to some form of Christianity. Their attendance at religious services also becomes more like that of those of their own age, which in many cases is less frequent than in their parents' experience.

At the same time, however, religious identity may become equally as important for children of immigrants as it was for their parents. Jeremy Lin, for example, kept very close to the Christian faith of his parents throughout his college years and now makes it a central part of his persona as an NBA player. In Europe (and to an extent in Canada), second-generation religious minorities attend services just as frequently as their parents' generation. Consequently, religion became a central issue of France's riots in 2005, even though most of the participants were born in France. All in all, it appears that the religious identity and practice of the second generation are rarely maintained in the same way as in their parents' faith. It is fluid, with faith becoming deeper for some immigrant children while less important for others.

Religious Organizations

The statistics in this book squarely focus on individual immigrants. Surveys of immigrants are mostly done in private and ask about their personal experiences. But immigrant religion is not entirely private. It is often practiced with others, mostly within religious organizations.

Studies show that religious organizations have helped migrants in moving to the new country. Although the people sent by religious organizations as religious ambassadors or missionaries represent a small portion of all the world's migrants, churches and other religious organizations in the home country often provide spiritual instruction and prayer for many immigrants before they leave. And once immigrants arrive, religious organizations are often the first groups to receive them. For example, the Buen Pastor church in North Carolina has been welcoming Protestant immigrants from Central America for years and has become a place of refuge and community for Latino immigrants.

Religious institutions not only provide immigrants with basic worship rites and lead them in spiritual experiences, but they also assist immigrants by offering a familiar place for ethnic groups to gather and help each other in their adjustment to the new country's society.[1] For example, the Christian faith of Jeremy Lin's family provided an environment where Jeremy was encouraged to reach high academic goals. Also, their church provided a location where a common set of beliefs and social networks could expand Jeremy's educational opportunities more than perhaps his parents could do on their own.

Statistics demonstrate that immigrants who attend religious services at religious organizations on a regular basis tend to have better mental and emotional health. It appears then that immigrants can find a personal refuge in religious organizations where their psychological needs can be met. But immigrants who are highly involved in religious organizations can also use their experience to become full members of society. For example, the Singh Multani family in Montreal used the support of their religious organization to help them in their legal battle. Their religious community not only offered legal assistance but also provided the moral and emotional support they needed to challenge the Montreal school board in court.

But it cannot be forgotten that the central character of the Singh Multani case was a child of immigrants, not an immigrant himself. In this way, religious organizations not only were part of his defense in helping him fight for the right to wear his ceremonial dagger to school, but Sikh religious organizations also culturally shaped his life, providing him a place where his faith was maintained.[2]

All of these examples demonstrate how religious organizations are influential in migration, the transformation of immigrant faith, and the role religious institutions can play in helping immigrants and their children adapt to their new environments.

Religious Contexts of Reception

Migrants do not move to destination countries devoid of religious histories, religious norms, and religious landscapes. So it is realistic to expect that immigrants will encounter many religious differences in the destination context compared with their countries of origin. The context of reception can play an important role in who moves where, how immigrants adapt their religion to their new surroundings, and how religion can help or hinder immigrant integration.

People move all over the world, but as this book has shown, many move to the Western world to countries like the United States, Canada, and Western Europe. Currently, no known laws limit the entry of immigrants into these countries on the basis of their religion. But this does not mean that religion is not a contributor to determining who enters.

For example, Gunbar Singh Multani's family is part of the Sikh community, a religious group from India. Several members of this religious group were admitted into Canada on the basis of their refugee status following a long and historical conflict between Sikhs and other religious groups in India. Although it is difficult to separate ethnicity and religion for this group, religion was certainly a part of the reason why this immigrant religious group grew in size in Canada and other countries. By contrast, a much smaller portion of other Indian religious groups came to the West on the basis of refugee status. Hindu and Christian Indians mostly migrated by other means, often as skilled workers or joining family already in the destination country.

Other examples demonstrate how religion indirectly influences which religious groups enter a particular country. For example, the United States granted asylum to many Iranians during the Islamic Revolution. Many of these immigrants had a weak connection to Islam, were part of a religious minority, or had no religious affiliation. During the Iraq War, many Christians were threatened, and some of them came to the United States; therefore, the Christian share of Iraqis in the United States is much higher than in Iraq as a whole. Although the United States may not have had a formal religion policy for immigration, other policies indirectly determined which religious groups were more likely to enter the United States from these countries. And over time, these selected religious groups continue to come to the United States through family connections.

But beyond the issues of who leaves and where they go, religious contexts of reception probably have more of an influence on the changing religion of immigrants. Immigrants adapt their frequency of religious attendance to that found in their new context. But, evidence also suggests that Muslim immigrants are more religious in areas of Europe where anti-immigrant sentiment is the highest. This correlation seems to imply that immigrants sensing hostility may respond with a religious reaction. For example, although it cannot be confirmed that the attention the Singh Multani family received from some hostile parents and school authorities over their son's predicament drove them to become more religious, it certainly framed the debate toward the adjudication of the issue as a matter of religious freedom.

Religious contexts of reception also shape the economic success of immigrants. Statistical patterns indicate that religious-minority immigrants and their adult children are less likely to be employed than the general public and Christian immigrants in Western Europe. It is possible that the historical connections between Christian religious groups through state-church relationships, as well as the high number of religious minorities that have entered Europe, set up a context where religious-minority immigrants (mostly Muslim in Europe) find it more difficult to find employment. Consequently, this can lead to fewer opportunities for religious minorities in some destination countries, even into the second generation. For example, the fact that unemployed, Muslim, second-generation youth in France rioted in 2005 demonstrates how differences in religious contexts can shape immigrant integration. By contrast, in the United States—a context where religion is separate from the state and most immigrants are Christian—almost all immigrant religious groups have an equal chance of succeeding economically, especially when other factors such as language and occupation are taken into account.

However, the United States was not always like this. Catholics were once regarded as a religious minority group distinctly different from the U.S. religious context, and their immigrant numbers were very large about a century ago. But, several generations later, Catholics have more or less entered the American mainstream, a testament to the rather equal opportunity for employment for America's latest Catholic immigrant group—Latinos from the south. Therefore, it appears that religious contexts of reception may also involve a time dimension, dependent on both the religious context and historical patterns of migration.

Religious contexts also shape the role of faith in the lives of second-generation immigrants. In France where the population is increasingly without a religious affiliation, any movement of second-generation youth away from their family's religion is often to the no-religious-affiliation category, while in the United States, second-generation immigrants switching religions may move from a non-Christian group to a Christian group or from a Christian group to no religious affiliation. Both Christians and those with no religion are sizeable groups within U.S. society. Also, children of immigrants with no religious heritage in the United States may eventually choose a religious affiliation as they adapt to a relatively more religious country.

Religious contexts also influence the intensity of religion for children of immigrants. For example, if Muslim children of immigrants were adapting to the religious environment in Europe, they would become less religious than their parents because religious attendance levels in

Europe are quite low compared to those in other contexts. But Muslim young adults in France who are identifiably choosing to remain attached to an Islamic identity show an opposite effect. Second-generation Muslims in Europe, on average, attend mosque just as frequently as their parents—a sign of religious resilience across generations. It is possible that the European religious context, which has not always been as welcoming to Muslims, contributes to a strengthened form of Islam among Muslim children of immigrants in Europe compared with those growing up in North America.

In sum, differences in religious contexts seem to be important for the movement of immigrants, changes to their faith, the role of faith in the integration of immigrants, and, finally, the transferring of faith into the second generation. Immigrant faith is dependent not only on immigrants themselves or which religious groups they belong to but also on the immigrants' new religious environment.

Religious Majorities and Religious Minorities

A final perspective on immigrant faith is religious majority (for the destination countries in this book, belonging to a Christian group) and religious minority (belonging to a religion that is not Christian) differences. Many of the issues of religious majorities and minorities have already been included in this concluding chapter, but it is worth mentioning some of the key areas again using a majority/minority framework, lest this important aspect of immigrant faith be overlooked.

Latino Protestants, like those of Buen Pastor Church in North Carolina, seem to be more likely to move to the United States than other religious groups. Indian Christians are a larger share of Indian immigrants in the United States than Indians as a whole. Iranians in the United States are not majority Muslim. All of these groups exemplify a common principle of migration and religion: minorities are more likely to move, and in many cases to move to places where their religious group is the majority or is larger than the proportional size in their country of origin. This means that on average, religious majorities can continue to grow in destination countries via migration while religious minorities in countries where emigration is significant may experience sharp declines.

The faith of religious minorities changes differently than the faith of religious majorities. Although both religious majority and religious minority groups seem to experience a sudden decline in religious attendance immediately following migration and immigrants of both groups soon adapt their frequency of attendance to the attendance levels of the general public in their local area, the religious-minority experience can be different in contexts where immigrants of certain ethnic or religious groups are experiencing anti-immigrant attitudes. Immigrant Muslims in Europe, for example, seem to have the highest religious attendance in areas where anti-immigrant sentiment is also the highest.

Children of immigrants belonging to religious minorities are less likely to shed their religious identity and involvement in religious organizations in contexts where religion is a barrier for integration. This is not the case in contexts like the United States, where religious-attendance levels of religious-minority children of immigrants look similar to the levels found in the general public. On the other hand, children of immigrants belonging to religious majorities are over time more likely to change religions and adapt their religious attendance levels to those of the general public, often becoming less religious than their parents' generation.

Religious majorities and minorities both seem to benefit psychologically from attending religious services, although religious-minority immigrants living in Europe and Canada (contexts where religion can be a barrier to integration) are happier when they attend religious services. Members of both groups regularly attending religious services also appear to be an active part of their new society, including becoming citizens and voting more frequently than nonattendees. But when it comes to economic success, religious minorities in contexts where religion is historically tied to the state seem to have a more difficult time finding a job and advancing their careers.

Although career advancement for children of immigrants belonging to religious minorities does not seem to be influenced by their religious affiliation, getting a job still seems to be a persistent problem for children of immigrants belonging to religious minorities in Europe. The French riots in 2005 are an example of how high levels of unemployment among Muslim youth can lead to unrest. On the flip side, religious majorities who regularly attend religious services have higher levels of education and experience greater career advancement. This religious-majority premium toward education and occupation seems to be most apparent in the United States but also appears to an extent in Canada, both places where religion is considered a bridge for immigrant integration. In this way, Jeremy Lin's success in graduating from a top university and in his career could be related to his high involvement with a religious organization.

Immigrant Faith: More Patterns and Trends to Come

The patterns presented in this book are only a beginning. In fact, the tapestry of immigrant religion has only begun to be woven. In the coming years, more religion measures and more details about immigrant religious groups will be forthcoming as additional data representing immigrant populations at large are collected. At the same time, new stories of immigrant faith will emerge, some being hidden from public view but some being part of the public conversation.

In the years ahead, additional data will allow us to identify more patterns, including trends over time. In some countries, children of immigrants belonging to religious minorities are only now becoming adults. Future surveys of this second-generation group will reveal whether the patterns and changes from one generation to the next are consistent with new religious groups. With immigration data becoming more reliable in many countries, describing religious trends in the flow of migrants to and from almost every country in the world will be more of a possibility. Moreover, as attitudes toward immigrants change in societies, patterns of immigrant faith may also change, some perhaps in line with those presented in this book, others with more nuanced differences.

Some patterns of immigrant faith remain less determined. One area that has received much discussion is immigrant religion and transnationalism. Much attention has surfaced on how religion has become a globalized field and is not limited to a single country or region.³ Migrants often become the carriers of religion and operate as the ties that bind cross-national religious movements together. Unfortunately, there is little quantitative data to connect the dots on this topic, either from immigrant surveys or from demographic data.

Another area to explore is whether the patterns of immigrant faith in the Western world can be applied to new immigrant destinations. Immigration has become an important issue for new destinations like Singapore, Hong Kong, Japan, and South Korea in East Asia, but also majority-Muslim countries in the Persian Gulf such as Saudi Arabia and Qatar. Many of these countries now have immigrant shares of their populations that exceed those found in many Western countries. Additionally, these new destinations are often not majority-Christian and contain migrants from countries typically not found in the West. We know very little about the religious lives of immigrants in these places. Stories of immigrant faith remain rather uncovered; statistical data are even less available.

Even with new destinations, new immigrant groups, and new ways of looking at immigrant religion, immigrant faith will remain an important part of the world's public conversation so long as people continue to cross international borders and religion is an important part of people's lives. To that end, this book represents only the first volume of a much larger story of immigrant faith—one section of an ever-growing tapestry.

Immigrant Faith presents various forms of qualitative and quantitative data. The reliability and validity of the data are discussed below.

Significance Testing

All significance testing for descriptive statistics are based on a 95 percent confidence interval. These tests are equivalent to t-tests between two groups (e.g., religious attendees vs. nonattendees, immigrants vs. children of immigrants) and can vary in significance by sample size for each group, the variance or spread of responses, and the mean distance in the estimates between the two groups. All data are based on demographic data or surveys; therefore, all numbers are considered estimates.

Selected Groups and Global Data Adjustments

Respondents are often divided into three groups: (1) foreign-born (immigrants), (2) those with at least one foreign-born parent (children of immigrants), and (3) those who are not foreign-born and do not have a foreign-born parent (general public). Differences between these synthetic immigrant generations do not necessarily represent change between generations. Some immigrants may have arrived only a few years ago while parents of children of immigrants could have arrived up to seventy-five years earlier.

Survey estimates of differences in education, employment, and occupation are limited to respondents who are ages twenty-five to sixty-four. Employment estimates are further limited to respondents in the labor market (have a job or are looking for a job). Occupation estimates include only employed respondents.

Some surveys asked respondents with no religious affiliation about their religious attendance while other surveys did not. To keep things consistent across datasets, religious attendance is considered to be less than monthly for respondents indicating no religious affiliation.

Peer-Reviewed Studies

The data analysis presented in the book is not always representative of immigrant populations. Much of it is derived from nationally representative social surveys in which certain immigrant groups may be less likely to participate. Also, the analyses are not statistically advanced. This is intentional so that an everyday reader can comprehend the material.

Nonetheless, for almost every section of the book, deeper-level analyses providing further evidence for a particular pattern can be found in one or more articles published by the author or colleagues in peer-reviewed journals. These articles are referenced in the endnotes and include various quantitative methods, including multivariate regression, multilevel regression, demographic comparisons, and additional robustness tests.

Demographic, Time, and Country Differences

Whenever possible, demographic differences by sex, age group, and ethnicity for findings in the book's tables and figures were compared. For the most part, there were few differences when analysis of the data occurred across major demographic groups. Differences for demographic groups where findings were statistically significant and different from those presented in the tables and figures are found in endnotes.

Many of the datasets also pool waves of surveys across several years and across several countries or states and provinces. As a robustness check, all patterns presented in *Immigrant Faith* were compared to the survey estimates after country/state/province of residence and year was controlled. No significant differences in patterns occurred when these geographic and time dimensions were taken into account.

Data

Immigrant stories presented throughout the chapters are based on true stories of acquaintances of the author. To protect the identity of these immigrants, pseudonyms have been used. These data were not systematically collected and is considered anecdotal. The purpose of the stories is to illustrate patterns seen in the quantitative data. Analysis based on demographic data and several surveys (immigrant and general population) are used in the tables and figures. Each dataset is described in the order it appears in the book. Each data source is briefly described, important alterations to the data are explained, and survey questions represented from the data are listed.

Pew Research Center's Global Religion and Migration Database

The Pew Research Center's Global Religion and Migration Database (GRMD) is a unique data source with an estimate by religion for every origin and destination country of international migrants. The data do not represent migrant flows, but migrant stocks or the total count of people living in a country where they were not born, in 2010. The data represent a snapshot in time of the total 215 million international migrants.

The GRMD was collected from various census and national statistical agencies throughout the world in 2010 and 2011. The data were then harmonized in 2012 following procedures adopted by the World Bank and the United Nations in preparing earlier waves of similar data. Origin data of all migrants in the world were collected first, followed by a religious distribution of migrants from and to every country in the world. The religion data were gathered from censuses and surveys in destination countries; but when religion data were unavailable, the origin country's religious composition was used as a proxy. For complete details of the data's methodology, see http://www.pewforum.org/Geography/ Religious-Migration-appendix-b.aspx. The dataset is publicly available at www.worldreligiondatabase.org.

World Values Survey Rounds 4 and 5

The World Values Survey (WVS) has been operating since the 1980s, surveying countries around the world with nationally representative surveys. Round 4's surveys occurred around the year 2000 while round 5's surveys happened around 2005.

Questions used from the World Values Survey include the following:

- Apart from weddings, funerals, and christenings, about how often do you attend religious services these days?
- On this list are various groups of people. Could you please indicate any that you would not like to have as neighbors? [answers include immigrants/foreign workers, people of a different religion]

All estimates use WVS's sampling weights and include the nonresponse category for missing data (don't know, no response). The dataset is publicly available at http://www.worldvaluessurvey.org.

New Immigrant Survey

The New Immigrant Survey (NIS) is a survey of new immigrants receiving permanent residency (or green cards) in the United States in 2003. About half of the approximately eighty-five hundred adult respondents adjusted their immigrant status while already living in the United States, while the other half came directly from their country of origin. Immigrants were interviewed about six months after receiving their permanent residency. Interviews for the first round (R1) were done in person, often at the respondent's residence.

The response rate was 68 percent, with interviews conducted in

English, Spanish, and seventeen other languages. The survey is representative of new legal permanent residents in 2003 with oversamples for refugee and diversity lottery applicants. The NIS is funded by a combination of government agencies and private foundations. Principal investigators include Guillermina Jasso (New York University), Douglas Massey (Princeton University), Mark Rosenzweig (Yale University), and James Smith (RAND Corporation). It is a multidisciplinary survey with modules on demographics, migration history, health, language, remittances, economics, and religion.

Round 2 (R2) surveyed the same immigrants approximately five years later with about half of the original group of respondents interviewed. There are no apparent demographic differences between the respondents in round 1 and those in round 2.

Questions used from the NIS include the following:

- R1: Before coming to the United States to live, how often did you attend religious services in your country of last foreign residence? [Response included a number of categories.]
- R1: Since becoming a permanent resident, how many times have you attended religious services? [Response was numeric, recoded into number of times per month.]
- R1 and R2: What religious tradition, if any, describes your current religion (you may mention more than one, if you wish)? [Christians include Catholic, Protestant, Christian Orthodox, and recoding of other responses that appear to be part of a Christian category, including Mormons and Jehovah's Witnesses. No religious affiliation was its own response category. Other religions included Muslim, Hindu, Buddhist, and other stated religions that did not fit within the Christian categorization.]
- R1: What religious tradition, if any, were you raised in (you may mention more than one, if you wish)?
- R2: When we last spoke, you described your religious tradition as _____. Does this still describe your current religion?
- R2: Do you intend to file to become a citizen?

More information about the NIS can be found at http://nis.princeton
.edu. Data used in *Immigrant Faith* are the restricted data files received
in 2007 (R1) and 2012 (R2).

Pew Research Center's Global Religious Landscape

The Pew Research Center's Global Religious Landscape is a demographic
study in which the religious composition of each country of the world
in 2010 is estimated. Sources include censuses, surveys, and historical information, used to derive the best possible religious estimate for
each country. More information on the methodology of this project
can be found at http://www.pewforum.org/global-religious-landscape
-methodology.aspx.

U.S. General Social Survey

The General Social Survey (GSS) in the United States is carried out by the
National Opinion Research Council at the University of Chicago and has
been conducted since 1972. The survey sample is nationally representative
and conducted biannually with more than two thousand respondents
each year. As part of the International Social Survey Program, the survey is designed to be comparable to other social surveys internationally.
Interviews are done face to face, and Spanish interviews began in 2006.

Due to the small number of cases for immigrants and particularly
immigrants and children of immigrants belonging to a religious minority
group, the data represent a pooled sample of respondents from 2000 to
2010. Fortunately, regression results indicate no statistically significant
differences when year of survey is controlled. To take internal variation
by geographic region into account, there were also no differences in estimates when region of residence is controlled.

Questions from the GSS used in *Immigrant Faith* include the following:

- Were you born in this country?

- Were both your parents born in this country? [separate responses for mother and father]
- What is your religious preference? Is it Protestant, Catholic, Jewish, some other religion, or no religion? [Protestant, Catholic, Christian Orthodox, Other Christian coded as Christian; all other religious groups coded as Other Religion]
- In what religion were you raised? [Protestant, Catholic, Christian Orthodox, Other Christian coded as Christian; all other religious groups coded as Other Religion]
- How often do you attend religious services? [categorical response; respondents with no religious affiliation coded as having no religious attendance]
- Last week were you working full time, part time, going to school, keeping house, or what?
- Taken all together, how would you say things are these days—would you say that you are very happy or not too happy?
- Occupation ISCO88 codes [ISCO88 codes less than 4000 considered professional occupations]
- Years of education [composite measure based on various questions regarding education and schooling; more than twelve years considered as some college or more]
- In 2008 [similar question for previous years and elections], you remember that Obama ran for President on the Democratic ticket against McCain for the Republicans. Do you remember for sure whether or not you voted in that election? [included only those stating they were eligible to vote]

All estimates use GSS's sampling weights and include the nonresponse category for missing data (don't know, no response). Data are publicly available at http://www3.norc.org/gss+website.

Ethnic Diversity Survey

The Ethnic Diversity Survey (EDS) was conducted by Statistics Canada in 2003. The EDS is a nationally representative sample of more than forty-two thousand respondents, excluding residents of institutions and those claiming an aboriginal ethnic origin. Two phases of sampling occurred: one among the general population, the second among members of the Canadian population indicating an ethnic origin other than Canadian, British Isles, French, American, or Australian/New Zealander. Because of this oversample of ethnic groups, many of the respondents were immigrants or children of immigrants. Telephone interviews were conducted in several languages with a final response rate of 76 percent. Foreign-born cases were divided by time of arrival to Canada (ten years or less or more than ten years).

Questions from the EDS used in *Immigrant Faith* include the following:

- In the past 12 months, how often did you participate in religious activities or attend religious services or meetings with other people, other than for events such as weddings and funerals? [categorical responses]
- In what year did you first come to Canada to live?
- In what country were you born?

All estimates use EDS's sampling weights and include the nonresponse category for missing data (don't know, no response). More information about the EDS can be found at http://www23.statcan.gc.ca/imdb/p2SV.pl ?Function=getSurvey&SDDS=4508&Item_Id=1717&lang=en.

European Social Survey

The European Social Survey (ESS) is an award-winning, nationally representative survey of several European countries. Surveys are conducted biannually in the national language(s) in face-to-face interviews, with about two thousand completed interviews in each country each year. Although each country conducts its own survey using a common questionnaire, the project as a whole is coordinated by the Centre for Comparative Social Surveys at City University London. The ESS has a nearly 70 percent response rate in most countries.

Due to the small number of cases for immigrants and children of immigrants, the data represent a pooled sample of respondents from 2002 to 2010. Fortunately, regression results indicate no statistically significant differences when year of survey is controlled. As for internal variation by geographic region into account, there are also no differences in estimates when country of residence is controlled.

For the purposes of analysis for *Immigrant Faith*, the ESS sample was restricted to the original fifteen European Union countries (Austria, Belgium, Denmark, Finland, France, Germany, Greece, Ireland, Italy, Luxembourg, the Netherlands, Portugal, Spain, Sweden, and the United Kingdom), plus Norway and Switzerland.

Questions from the ESS used in *Immigrant Faith* include the following:

- Were you born in [country]? In which country were you born?
- Was your father born in [country]? In which country was your father born? Was your mother born in [country]? In which country was your mother born?
- Apart from special occasions such as weddings and funerals, about how often do you attend religious services nowadays?
- And which of these descriptions best describes your situation (in the last seven days)? [Categorical responses included in paid work, in education, unemployed and actively looking for a job, unemployed and wanting a job but not actively looking for a job, permanently sick or disabled, retired, in community or military service, doing housework, other.]
- What year did you first come to live in [country]?
- Do you consider yourself as belonging to any particular religion or denomination? [If respondent says yes, follow up is, Which one?]
- Taking all things together, how happy would you say you are? [0 to 10 scale; 8 or higher coded as very happy]
- What is the highest level of education you have successfully completed? [categorical responses; lower and higher tertiary education considered as some college or more]
- Occupation coded as ISCO88 codes based on the following questions: What

is/was the name or title of your main job? In your main job, what kind of work do/did you do most of the time? What training or qualifications are/were needed for the job? [ISCO88 codes less than 4000 considered professional occupations]

- Some people don't vote nowadays for one reason or another. Did you vote in the last [country] national election in [month/year]?
- Are you a citizen of [country]?
- Would you say that [country]'s cultural life is generally undermined or enriched by people coming to live here from other countries? [1 to 10 scale; 0 = cultural life undermined, 10 = cultural life enriched]

All estimates use a combination weight of ESS population and sampling design weights and include the nonresponse category for missing data (don't know, no response). More information and data downloads for the ESS can be found at http://www.europeansocialsurvey.org.

UK Understanding Society Survey

The UK Understanding Society Survey (UKSoc) is a longitudinal, nationally representative survey of forty thousand households across the UK. The data for *Immigrant Faith* were drawn from the first wave of the survey conducted from January 2009 to December 2010. Minority ethnic groups are oversampled, leading to a greater number of first- and second-generation immigrants and thus religious minorities. Interviews were conducted face to face, with translations available in nine additional languages besides English. The effort is led by the Institute for Social and Economic Research at the University of Essex and is funded by the Economic and Social Research Council.

Questions from the UKSoc used in *Immigrant Faith* include the following:

- Do you regard yourself as belonging to any particular religion? What is your religion, even if you are not practising?

- How often, if at all, do you attend religious services or meetings? [categorical response]
- In which country were you born?
- In which country was your mother born? In which country was your father born?

All estimates use UKSoc's sampling weights and include the nonresponse category for missing data (don't know, no response). More information about the USoc can be found at https://www.understandingsociety.ac.uk.

Germany Generations and Gender Survey

Germany's Generations and Gender Survey (GGS) was conducted in 2005, interviewing both German citizens (more than ten thousand interviews consisting of a variety of religious groups) and Turkish noncitizens (more than four thousand interviews and almost entirely Muslim). Interviews for the German sample were conducted in German while the Turkish interviews were performed in Turkish. Samples of each group are considered nationally representative. The study is part of a cross-national effort to survey European populations on topics related to demographic change and is sponsored by the United Nations Economic Commission for Europe.

Since the two samples of German citizens and Turkish noncitizens cannot be combined, Muslims in the citizen sample were removed and not combined with the noncitizen sample. Christians with a migrant background (either first or second generation) are drawn from the citizen sample. This structure of the data could bias findings in that more acculturated Christian immigrants (because they are citizens) are included in the sample while less acculturated Muslim immigrants (because they are noncitizens) are also included.

Questions from the GGS used in *Immigrant Faith* include the following:

- In which country were you born?

- In which country was your father born? In which country was your mother born?
- Which religious denomination do you adhere to, if any?
- How often, if at all, do you attend religious services (apart from weddings, funerals, baptisms, and the like)? [times per week, month, or year, recoded to monthly or more frequently]

All estimates use GGS's sampling weights and include the nonresponse category for missing data (don't know, no response). More information about the GGS can be found at http://www.ggp-i.org.

Trajectoires et Origines Survey

France's Trajectoires et Origines (TeO) survey of more than twenty-one thousand interviews was conducted in 2007 by the L'institut nationale d'études démographiques (INED) and L'institut national de la statistique et des etudes économiques (INSEE). The study employed separate sampling frames for first- and second-generation immigrants as well as the nonmigrant French population. The emphasis of the survey was to measure differences of integration and discrimination across the three groups; therefore, a large number of interviews were conducted among first- and second-generation immigrants.

Questions from the TeO used in *Immigrant Faith* include the following:

- Do you attend religious services? [categorical response]
- Do you currently have a religion? Which one?
- Does your father have a religion? Which one? / Does your mother have a religion? Which one? [religion raised coded as the religion of both parents if shared the same religious affiliation]

All estimates use TeO's sampling weights and include the nonresponse category for missing data (don't know, no response). More information about the TeO can be found at http://teo_english.site.ined.fr.

Canada General Social Survey

Statistics Canada has conducted a nationally representative general social survey (CGSS) on various topics each year since 1985. Each survey consists of a core module of questions, in which religious affiliation and religious attendance are always included. The CGSS is conducted in English and French to more than twenty-five thousand Canadians each year, averaging a response rate around 70 percent each year.

Since the number of immigrants belonging to religious minority groups is small in any individual survey, several surveys across different years are pooled together. Survey years were selected on the basis of their representativeness of the country as a whole and variables available for analysis.

Questions from CGSS used in *Immigrant Faith* include the following:

- What, if any, is your religion?
- Other than on special occasions (such as weddings, funerals, or baptisms), how often did you attend religious services or meetings in the last 12 months? Was it: at least once a week? at least once a month? a few times a year? at least once a year? not at all?
- In what country were you born?
- In what country was your mother born?
- In what country was your father born?
- Think of all the friends you had contact with in the past month, whether the contact was in person, by telephone, or by e-mail. Of all these people, how many have the same mother tongue as you? [all, most, and about half codes as different-language friends]
- Think of all the friends you had contact with in the past month, whether the contact was in person, by telephone, or by e-mail. Of all these people, how many come from an ethnic group that is visibly different from yours? [all, most, and about half codes as different-ethnic friends]
- Highest level of education obtained by the respondent. [Some university/ community college or higher coded as some college or more.]

- Main activity of the respondent in the last 12 months. [Working at a paid job or business and looking for paid work coded as part of labor force.]
- Occupation: Standard Occupational Classification (1991) of the respondent—10 categories [classifications at level five or less coded as professional occupations]
- Range of years when the respondent came to live permanently in Canada.

All estimates use CGSS sampling weights and include the nonresponse category for missing data (don't know, no response). The CGSS analysis was drawn from Statistics Canada microdata files of the Canadian General Social Surveys, which contain anonymized data for years 2000 through 2009. All computations on these microdata were prepared by the author and the responsibility for the use and interpretation of these data are entirely that of the author(s). More information about the CGSS, including data accessibility, can be found at http://www5.statcan.gc.ca/bsolc/olc-cel/olc-cel?catno=89F0115X&CHROPG=1&lang=eng.

Longitudinal Survey of Immigrants to Canada

The Longitudinal Survey of Immigrants to Canada (LSIC) is a representative sample of new arrivals to Canada in 2001 aged fifteen years or older who entered Canada as permanent residents through a Canadian Mission Abroad. More than twelve thousand face-to-face interviews were conducted in fifteen languages. Immigrants were interviewed again in 2003 and 2005. However, the religious-attendance question changed in 2005, allowing for no additional trends beyond the 2003 time point.

Questions from the LSIC used in *Immigrant Faith* include the following:

- What is your religion?
- Are you a member, or have you taken part in the activities of any groups or organizations in Canada (for example: a religious group, ethnic association, sports club, etc.)?

- What kinds of groups or organizations were they? [church or religious group one option of many] How frequently do you take part in "group" activities? [categorical response]

LSIC data were accessed June 2008 through April 2010 at the Quebec Inter-University Centre for Social Statistics, Montreal, Canada. Consequently, the views, opinions, and analysis expressed in this book reflect the researcher and not Statistics Canada. More information about the Longitudinal Survey of Immigrants to Canada can be found at http://www23.statcan.gc.ca/imdb/p2SV.pl?Function=getSurvey &SDDS=4422&Item_Id=1479&lang=en#a4.

Pew Research Center's Asian American Survey

The Pew Research Center's Asian American Survey was conducted in 2012, interviewing more than thirty-five hundred Asian Americans aged eighteen years or older living in the United States. The survey is nationally representative of all fifty states. The survey was designed to sufficiently sample individual Asian subgroups, including Chinese, Filipinos, Asian Indians, Japanese, Koreans, and Vietnamese. Respondents were selected on the basis of a combination of screening for Asian Americans, using name-based lists, and recontacting self-identified Asians from previous Pew Research surveys. Surveys were conducted in Mandarin, Cantonese, Korean, Vietnamese, Japanese, Hindu, and Tagalog.

Questions from the Asian American survey used in *Immigrant Faith* include the following:

- What is your present religion, if any? Are you Protestant, Roman Catholic, Mormon, Orthodox such as Greek or Russian Orthodox, Jewish, Muslim, Buddhist, Hindu, atheist, agnostic, something else, or nothing in particular?
- Now thinking about when you were a child, in what religion were you raised, if any? Were you Protestant, Roman Catholic, Mormon, Orthodox such

as Greek or Russian Orthodox, Jewish, Muslim, Buddhist, Hindu, atheist, agnostic, something else, or nothing in particular?

- In what country were you born?
- In what country was your father born? In what country was your mother born?

All estimates use Pew Research sampling weights and include the nonresponse category for missing data (don't know, no response). More information about the Asian American survey can be found at http://www .pewsocialtrends.org/2012/06/19/the-rise-of-asian-americans.

NOTES

NOTES TO THE INTRODUCTION

1. For more information on this news story see Bob Geary, "Case Closed," *Indy Week*, Sept. 18, 2012, available at http://www.indyweek.com/citizen/archives/2012/09/18/case-closed-two-years-later-remaining-buen-pastor-defendants-free-of-deportation-threat, downloaded January 2013.

2. Marcus Thompson II, "Exclusive: Jeremy Lin Says 'Lin-sanity' Was Triggered by a Leap of Faith," *San Jose Mercury News*, Feb. 13, 2012, available at http://www.webcitation.org/65QguzbVh.

3. Immigrant societies are constantly changing. For example, about one hundred years ago, many in the United States were hostile toward the millions of Catholic immigrants entering the country at the time. Today, the presence of the Catholic Church in the United States does not lead to such highly negative public opinion. Other historical examples in Canada and Western Europe demonstrate how immigrants and their religions change societies as boundaries of difference get blurred (see Alba 2005). *Immigrant Faith* does not present a historical account; instead, it reflects current reality in the United States, Canada, and Western Europe. The general patterns may not exist indefinitely as these societies are inevitably changed by the presence of immigrants. More important to understanding immigrant religion is the way elements of a given context can lead to differences in immigrant religion, regardless of geographic location.

4. Defining religion has been an important task among scholars in the humanities and the social sciences. In relying on just a few religion variables in several datasets, this book does not aim to exhaustively look at the meaning of religion in immigrant lives. Nor does the book interrogate how immigrant faith adds to our understanding of religion. Although it would be instructive to analyze more religion variables, there are inadequate data with which to do so.

5. For more information on immigrant religion and public policy see Bramadat and Koenig 2009; Breton 2012.

NOTES TO CHAPTER 1

1. Stories appearing in the book are based on true stories from the author's personal interaction with immigrants. To protect the identity of immigrants, names of individuals and some locations have been changed.

2. Population counts and percentages for the world's migrants are for international

migrant stock in 2010 (living, foreign-born people who have lived for at least one year in a country where they were not born). Estimates are taken from the Pew Research Center's Global Religion and Migration Database. For more information on the database and its corresponding report, *Faith on the Move*, see http://www .pewforum.org/faith-on-the-move.aspx.

3. "Europe" and "Western Europe" are used interchangeably and refer to the fifteen European Union countries prior to the 2004 enlargement, plus Norway and Switzerland.

4. About half of new permanent residents already live in the United States. For U.S. immigration statistics, see the Department of Homeland Security's website at http://www.dhs.gov/immigration-statistics.

5. For Canada's immigration statistics, see Citizenship and Immigration Canada's website at http://www.cic.gc.ca/english/resources/statistics/index.asp.

6. For a good discussion of differing views of immigrants in the United States and Europe, see Zolberg and Woon 1999.

7. In fact, more Muslims in Europe view themselves as Muslim first, above their nationality. See the Pew Research Center's 2006 report at http://www.pewglobal .org/2006/07/06/muslims-in-europe-economic-worries-top-concerns-about -religious-and-cultural-identity.

8. Gorski 2003; Tilly 1990.

9. For a discussion on how the European immigrant became identified as Muslim, see Allievi 2005.

10. Canada is argued to be a religious context exhibiting qualities both like the United States and like Europe; see Lyon and Van Die 2000.

11. For a good overview of religion and immigration issues in Canada, see Breton 2012.

12. Castles and Miller 2003; Portes and Rumbaut 2006.

13. Massey et al. 1998.

14. Among Indians moving to the United States, a substantial number were Malayalee nurses and their families from Kerala, a region of India that is heavily Christian; see George 2005.

15. Data are from various surveys and censuses included in the Pew Research Center's Global Religion and Migration Database (2012) for international migrant stock in 2010. Although it is possible that the larger-than-expected percentages of Christians is due to religious switching after migration, switching between major world religions is quite rare among immigrants (see chapter 2).

16. An interactive map of immigrants by country of origin and destination, all by religion, can be found at http://www.pewforum.org/faith-on-the-move.aspx.

17. Connor 2012b.

18. Pedersen and Dalen 2007.

19. Immigrant religious minority/majority status in their country of origin and country of destination can also affect religiosity; see Yang and Ebaugh 2001.

20. Finke and Stark 1992, 33–35.
21. More information about the New Immigrant Survey can be found at www.nis .princeton.edu.
22. Immigrants express their religious beliefs in other ways than by attending religious services, including personal prayer, believing in a set of theological doctrines, practicing meditation, abstaining from certain behaviors, and committing acts of service. However, this type of data is not regularly asked for in many surveys of immigrants. Thus, most of the tables and charts in this book use religious attendance as a proxy for religiosity. Despite this religious measure's shortcomings, religious attendance is nonetheless highly correlated with other measures of religiosity regardless of religious affiliation; see Norris and Inglehart 2004.
23. Monthly or more often is one of the obvious cut-points that are consistent across the two datasets. A weekly-or-more frequency provides similar findings.
24. Although the different wording of the religious-attendance question in the two surveys could introduce some measurement bias, further analysis controlling for several socio-demographic variables presents a similarly mixed picture; see Connor 2009.
25. Meyer 2000.
26. Handlin 1973 [1951], 93.
27. Hagan 2008, 156.
28. People living in more insecure environments are theorized to be more religious; see Norris and Inglehart 2004.
29. Smith 1978.
30. Portes and Rumbaut 2006, 92–93.
31. Pew Research Center 2012, 53.
32. Koopmans argues that the relatively larger percentage of Muslims in European countries compared with other Western countries has led to a lower value for multicultural societies in European destinations; see Koopmans 2013.
33. For a description of prominent immigrant faiths in the past, see Herberg 1960. For a good overview of how these immigrant faiths became part of mainstream American society, see Alba, Raboteau, and DeWind 2009.
34. For more information on MIPEX or to download data, see http://www.mipex.eu.
35. Religious favoritism scores by country can be found at the Pew Research Center's Religion & Public Life Project at http://www.pewforum.org/uploadedFiles/Topics/ Issues/Government/Results-by-Country.pdf.
36. Connor and Koenig 2013.
37. Foner and Alba 2008.

NOTES TO CHAPTER 2

1. Evidence of internal migration within the United States indicates lower religious attendance among Americans who move. See Smith, Sikink, and Bailey 1998.
2. One exception is those with no religious affiliation. Their participation in religious

services actually increased slightly after they arrived in the United States—a possible indicator of religious adaptation to a more religious context than their country of origin.

3. Throughout the book, the U.S. statistics remain generally the same even when Mexicans (nearly a third of all immigrants in the United States) are not included. Also, statistics for all countries were separated for men and women with still no major differences than those presented for both sexes.

4. Kurien 2002; Cassanova 2007.

5. For review, see Hirschman 2004.

6. Connor 2008; Diehl and Koenig 2013; Van Tubergen 2013.

7. Internal migrants within the United States have lower religious attendance than those who do not move in the United States. See Wuthow and Christiano 1979.

8. Immigrant fertility commonly falls after migration, later adapting to the immigrant's new context; see Stephen and Bean 1992.

9. Connor 2009.

10. From a multiculturalist perspective, see Glazer 1997. For an assimilation perspective, see Gordon 1964. Middle-ground perspectives involve selective acculturation where some groups adapt more quickly than others, depending on their local context, how they are viewed by the general public, and the type of family support available. For more details, see Portes and Rumbaut 2006.

11. Park and Burgess 1921 [1969].

12. This view is documented by Warner 1994. For more examples of immigrant congregation studies, see Ebaugh and Chafetz 2000; Warner and Wittner 1998; Carnes and Yang 2004; Guest 2003.

13. There is a notable exception among Buddhist immigrants; see Cadge 2008.

14. For more information on Muslim networks in Europe, see Pew Research Center 2010.

15. Voas and Fleischmann 2012.

16. Eisen 2009.

17. Dusenbery 1992.

18. Chen argues that in becoming religious in the relatively religious country of the United States, immigrants become American; see Chen 2008.

19. O'Toole 1996.

20. Time in country can also reflect differences between immigrants arriving in different years, otherwise known as cohort effects. In other words, non-Christian immigrants arriving in the United States more than ten years before the survey could have been less religious than non-Christian immigrants arriving later.

21. For a good overview of immigration history during this time period, see Higham 2007 [1955]. For examples of Catholic religiosity during this time, see Handlin 1973 [1951]; Thomas and Znaniecki 1996; Dolan 1972.

22. Alba and Orsi 2008.

23. Herberg 1960, 27–28.

24. Guo Kai Li's deepening faith in an atmosphere of hostility toward her religion is similar to the sentiments experienced by evangelicals in the United States; see Smith and Emerson 1998.

25. Zolberg and Woon 1999.

26. Alba 2005; Foner and Alba 2008.

27. Portes and Rumbaut 2006, 325–31.

28. Pew Research Center 2011.

29. The growth of anti-immigrant attitudes in Europe is part of a growing right-wing political movement; see Norris 2005.

30. These brief findings are drawn from a more in-depth study; see Connor 2010.

31. Several studies correlate attitudes toward immigrants with immigrant outcomes. For example, see De Jong and Steinmetz 2004.

32. Notable studies on religious conversion among immigrants include Chen 2008; Yang 1999.

33. Unfortunately, the NIS data in the United States do not permit analysis of denominational switching within a given religious group. Nor are similar data available for immigrants in Canada.

34. The United States is now estimated to be a plurality of religious groups with Protestantism representing just under half of the population.

35. Although the majority of France's population is Catholic, the affiliation is more a matter of name than of practice. The society is heavily secular; see Koussens 2009.

36. Skirbekk et al. 2012.

37. It is possible that small degrees of religious switching for some groups can lead to even more switching as time goes on or involve a large number of people when origin groups are quite large. Qualitative evidence among Chinese Americans seems to be an example of such a case. See Yang 1999; Guest 2003; Chen 2008.

38. Further analysis of the New Immigrant Survey found that on average, even immigrants living in the United States for several years had not regained the frequency of religious attendance they had in their home country.

NOTES TO CHAPTER 3

1. The use of France as an example does not necessarily mean it is indicative for all of Western Europe. Each country has a history of integrating immigrants differently. Also, immigrant integration policies differ across European countries. See Crul, Schneider, and Lelie 2012 as an example. Whenever possible, distinctive differences seen in data or in comparative research in Western Europe are noted.

2. Mohammed's story actually took place in Montreal, Quebec, also a transportation production center and the world's second-largest francophone city. The province of Quebec also has some similarities to France in the way religion helps or hinders immigrant integration (Mooney 2009). Both France and Quebec have low attendance rates, are the recipients of many Muslim immigrants from North Africa, and have largely dispelled religion from having a prominent role within society.

Despite the change in location, all other facts of the story are accurate. Given that many of the findings for the role of religion in immigrant integration are similar in Canada and Europe, the change in location is not totally unjustified. The location in the story was changed to Toulouse to allow for a story from Europe and was done so for illustrative rather than factual purposes.

3. For a good overview of integration from an analytical view of assimilation, see chapters 1 and 2 of Alba and Nee 2003.

4. Immigrant integration is a controversial area of discussion within scholarship. In times past, there was the expectation that immigrants adjust to mainstream society through a process of assimilation; see Gordon 1964. Later on, multiculturalism became the more dominant perspective; see Glazer 1993. Today, assimilation has regained prominence once more, but more as an analytical term than as a normative one; see Brubaker 2001.

5. The terms "refuge," "resources," and "respect" are borrowed from Charles Hirschman's typology found in Hirschman 2004.

6. For a theoretical discussion of the bridge/barrier metaphor, see Foner and Alba 2008.

7. For more on the comparison of being Muslim in Europe and Spanish-speaking in the United States, see Zolberg and Woon 1999.

8. The important role of religion within the civic life of the United States was first documented by de Tocqueville 2000 [1835].

9. Robert Putnam and David Campbell describe religious organizations as a central part of American civil society; see Putnam and Campbell 2010.

10. For more on how immigrant religion can be a barrier in European societies with an official church-state relationship, see Fetzer and Soper 2005.

11. In 2006, Pew Research Center found that 49 percent of Great Britain was very concerned about the future of Muslims in their country while about 31 percent was somewhat concerned. Similar levels of concern about Muslims were also found in France, Spain, and Germany; see http://www.pewglobal.org/2006/07/06/muslims -in-europe-economic-worries-top-concerns-about-religious-and-cultural-identity.

12. See European analysis of immigrants in the Pew Research Center's report, *Faith on the Move*, http://www.pewforum.org/faith-on-the-move.aspx.

13. Mooney 2009; Koussens 2009.

14. Adida, Latin, and Valfort 2010.

15. For a deeper discussion of how Canada is both a bridge and a barrier for immigrant integration, see Connor and Koenig 2013.

16. Other integration outcomes such as language and physical health are not included in these analyses because data are either more limited for these outcomes or when available do not contain significant differences by religious group or religious attendance.

17. Peter Berger describes religion as being a theodicy, helping people understand difficult life situations in light of some kind of religious purpose; see Berger 1967.

18. For more information on the factors leading to anxiety among immigrants and how religion can relieve these ills, see Portes and Rumbaut 2006 (chapter 9 on religion).

19. For a discussion of how immigrants use religion as a means to protect their children from American or European values that are in disagreement with their own, see Kurien 2002; Dietz and El-Shouhoumi 2002.

20. Mooney 2009.

21. Unfortunately, the measures for depression across countries are different and cannot be easily presented; for more information on these findings, see Connor 2012a.

22. Harker 2001; Gozdziak 2002.

23. There may be instances where immigrants do not desire to integrate all areas of their lives. Also, integration into society is not always positive. Integration analysis in this chapter is not meant to condone a normative view of adaptation, but rather represents an analytical perspective as described by Brubaker 2001 and Alba and Nee 2003.

24. These findings are similar to the lack of differences in employment by religion in a recent survey of U.S. immigrants; see Connor 2011.

25. Koenig and Connor 2013.

26. Another study using a survey of immigrants arriving in the United States in 2003 shows a similar pattern: religion makes little difference in immigrant mobility at work when education is taken into account; see Connor 2011.

27. However, there remain a few caveats before this conclusion can be fully asserted. First, Western Europe is a large geographic zone with each country having unique social, religious, and political histories. It could be expected that the patterns found in Europe regarding immigrant religious minorities and employment could vary from country to country. However, further analysis of data with an even greater number of immigrants in France, Great Britain, and Germany indicates a similar story, particularly for Muslim immigrants. In all three countries, Muslim immigrants were less likely to be employed than the general public and Christian immigrants, even when other variables were factored in. In terms of occupational mobility, the gap between Muslim immigrants and Christian immigrants was still significant, but not as large as it was for employment.

    Another piece of the religious-minority puzzle is that being a Muslim or part of another non-Christian religion in Europe could be a proxy for being an ethnic minority. Often, the two aspects of ethnicity and religion go hand in hand for immigrants. However, additional research demonstrates that ethnicity does not seem to be the underlying issue, neither for employment nor for occupational mobility. Further analysis of immigrants across Europe indicates that being Muslim is a significant predictor for lower employment even when country of origin is taken into account. And further analysis comparing immigrant Muslims from different origin countries to different destination countries (Turks in Germany, South Asians in Great Britain, North Africans in France) indicates similar patterns in employment and occupation as those presented for all of Europe.

28. Putnam 2000. For an alternative way of defining social capital and its related effects, see Portes 2000.

29. See Putnam 2007. For a different view of Putnam's analysis, see Portes and Vickstom 2011.

30. Contact with different ethnic or language friends can mean all kinds of intergroup contact; consequently, it is difficult to accurately pinpoint the form or extent of contact. However, religion was found to have a largely indifferent influence on other measures of social integration in Canada; see Reitz et al. 2009.

31. This was found to be true in immigrant congregation studies; see Foley and Hoge 2007; Kniss and Numrich 2007.

32. For a more detailed analysis of this argument, see Orsi and Alba 2009.

33. George 1998.

34. This is the thesis of an in-depth study of immigrant congregations in the United States; see Kniss and Numrich 2007.

35. Unfortunately, the data do not allow us to tease apart whether religious attendance leads to U.S. citizenship or U.S. citizenship leads to higher religious attendance. It could also be possible that religious attendees simply carry a joiner attitude and are also more likely to join their new country of residence as a citizen.

36. Citizenship laws for immigrants vary considerably across Europe, with Germany permitting foreign-born residents of certain countries to naturalize only in recent years. For a more elaborate discussion of citizenship differences within Europe, see Brubaker 1992.

NOTES TO CHAPTER 4

1. Many immigrants speak of their disdain for the moral relativism found in Western societies and of the way religion can help their children's morals. Examples include Kurien 2001; Gibb and Rothenberg 2000; Dietz 2010.

2. For a more detailed discussion, see Alba and Nee 2003; Kasinitz et al. 2008.

3. Herbert Gans refers to "bumpy" assimilation when describing ups and downs in the adaptation of subsequent immigrant generations; see Gans 1999.

4. Sometimes there are examples when subsequent generations are not able to become part of mainstream society, particularly when it comes to economic status; see the Latino example in the United States in Telles and Ortiz 2008.

5. For more information on religious change in the second generation among individual religious groups, see Chen and Jeung 2012; Min 2010. For a more theoretical treatment of how second-generation immigrants adapt in a more segmented fashion due to individual and contextual factors, see Portes and Rumbaut 2001. For a discussion of how this segmented approach to adaptation shapes religious activity among the second generation, see Warner 2007.

6. In fact, the percentages of children of immigrants with no religious affiliation is of a similar range as that found among young adults in the United States; therefore it does not appear that children of immigrants are leaving religion in general

any more frequently than other American peers with no migration background. For more information on the growing number of religious "nones" in the United States, see the Pew Research Center's report, *Nones on the Rise*, http://www.pewforum.org/Unaffiliated/nones-on-the-rise.aspx.

7. For more information on religious switching in the United States see the Pew Research Center's report, *Faith in Flux*, http://www.pewforum.org/Faith-in-Flux.aspx.

8. This steadiness in religious attendance across immigrant generations among minority religious groups in Europe, most of which are Muslim, has been demonstrated by a number of studies in several European countries; see Lewis and Kashyap 2013; Jacob and Kalter 2013.

9. Immigrants with more social contact with nonimmigrants are less religious in the Netherlands; see Van Tubergen 2007.

10. Heath, Rothon, and Kilpi 2008.

11. One notable exception in postsecondary educational attainment is second-generation Muslims in Germany; see Crul et al. 2012.

12. See chapter on religion in Portes and Rumbaut 2006. Also see Park 2012; Bankston and Zhou 1995.

13. Unfortunately there is an insufficient number of non-Christian, second-generation immigrants ages twenty-five to sixty-four belonging to other religions in the US General Social Survey to display reliable percentages.

14. Koenig and Connor 2013.

15. The positive relationship between religious attendance among other religions in Canada and occupational attainment is contrary to findings in a previous article; see Connor and Koenig 2013. Once other factors are considered, the religious-attendance premium only occurs for Christian children of immigrants.

NOTES TO THE CONCLUSION

1. Several historical and comparative examples can be found in Alba, Raboteau, and DeWind 2009.

2. Read about the life cycle of an ethnic congregation in Mullins 1987.

3. Levitt 2007.

BIBLIOGRAPHY

Adida, Claire L., David D. Latin, and Marie-Anne Valfort. 2010. Identifying Barriers to Muslim Integration in France. *Proceedings of the National Academy of Sciences of the United States of America* 107 (52): 22384–90.

Alba, Richard. 2005. Bright vs. Blurred Boundaries: Second-Generation Assimilation and Exclusion in France, Germany, and the United States. *Ethnic and Racial Studies* 28 (1): 20–49.

Alba, Richard, and Victor Nee. 2003. *Remaking the American Mainstream: Assimilation and Contemporary Immigration.* Cambridge, MA: Harvard University Press.

Alba, Richard, and Robert Orsi. 2008. Passages in Piety: Generational Transitions and the Social and Religious Incorporation of Italian Americans. In *Immigration and Religion in America: Comparative and Historical Perspectives*, edited by R. Alba, A. J. Raboteau, and J. DeWind. New York: New York University Press.

Alba, Richard, Albert Raboteau, and Josh DeWind, eds. 2009. *Religion and Immigration in America: Comparative and Historical Perspectives.* New York: New York University Press.

Allievi, Stefano. 2005. How the Immigrant Has Become Muslim: Public Debates on Islam in Europe. *Revue europeenne des migrations internationales* 21 (2): 135–63.

Bankston, Carl L., and Min Zhou. 1995. Religious Participation, Ethnic Identification, and Adaptation of Vietnamese Adolescents in an Immigrant Community. *Sociological Quarterly* 36:523–34.

Berger, Peter. 1967. *The Sacred Canopy: Elements of a Sociological Theory of Religion.* New York: Anchor Books.

Bramadat, Paul, and Matthias Koenig. 2009. *International Migration and the Governance of Religious Diversity.* Montreal: McGill-Queen's University Press.

Breton, Raymond. 2012. *Different Gods: Integrating Non-Christian Minorities into a Primarily Christian Society.* Montreal: McGill-Queen's University Press.

Brubaker, Rogers. 1992. *Citizenship and Nationhood in France and Germany.* Cambridge, MA: Harvard University Press.

———. 2001. The Return of Assimilation? Changing Perspectives on Immigration and Its Sequels in France, Germany, and the United States. *Ethnic and Racial Studies* 24 (4): 531–48.

Cadge, Wendy 2008. De Facto Congregationalism and the Religious Organizations of Post-1965 Immigrants to the United States: A Revised Approach. *Journal of the American Academy of Religion* 76 (2): 344–74.

Carnes, Tony, and Fenggang Yang, eds. 2004. *Asian American Religons: The Making and Remaking of Borders and Boundaries*. New York: New York University Press.

Cassanova, Jose. 2007. Rethinking Secularization: A Global Comparative Perspective. In *Globalization, Religion, and Culture*, edited by P. Beyer and L. Beaman. Leiden: Brill.

Castles, Stephen, and Mark. J. Miller. 2003. *The Age of Migration: International Population Movements in the Modern World*, 3rd edition. New York: Guilford Press.

Chen, Carolyn. 2008. *Getting Saved in America: Taiwanese Immigration and Religious Experience*. Princeton, NJ: Princeton University Press.

Chen, Carolyn, and Russell Jeung, eds. 2012. *Sustaining Faith Traditions: Race, Ethncity, and Religion among the Latino and Asian American Second Generation*. New York: New York University Press.

Connor, Phillip. 2008. Increase or Decrease? The Impact of the International Migratory Event on Immigrant Religious Participation. *Journal for the Scientific Study of Religion* 47 (2): 243–57.

———. 2009. International Migration and Religious Participation: The Mediating Impact of Individual and Contextual Effects. *Sociological Forum* 24 (4): 779–803.

———. 2010. Contexts of Immigrant Receptivity and Immigrant Religious Outcomes: The Case of Muslims in Western Europe. *Ethnic and Racial Studies* 33 (3): 376-403.

———. 2011. Religion as Resource: Religion and Immigrant Economic Incorporation. *Social Science Research* 40 (5): 1350–61.

———. 2012a. Balm for the Soul: Immigrant Religion and Emotional Well-Being. *Internatinal Migration* 50 (2): 130–57.

———. 2012b. International Migration and Religious Selection. *Journal for the Scientific Study of Religion* 51 (1): 184–94.

Connor, Phillip, and Matthias Koenig. 2013. Bridges and Barriers: Religion and Immigrant Occupational Attainment across Integration Contexts. *International Migration Review* 47 (1): 3–38.

Crul, Maurice, Jens Schneider, and Frans Lelie, eds. 2012. *The European Second Generation Compared: Does Integration Context Matter?* Amsterdam: Amsterdam University Press.

Crul, Maurice, Philipp Schnell, Barbara Herzog-Punzenberger, Maren Wilmes, Marieke Slootman, and Rosa Aparicio Gomex. 2012. School Careers of Second-Generation Youth in Europe. In *The European Second Generation Compared*, edited by M. Crul, J. Schneider, and F. Lelie. Amsterdam: Amsterdam University Press.

De Jong, Gordon F., and Michele Steinmetz. 2004. Receptivity Attitudes and the Occupational Attainment of Male and Female Immigrant Workers. *Population Research and Policy Review* 23:91–116.

de Tocqueville, Alexis. 2000 [1835]. *Democracy in America*. Translated by H. Reeve. New York: Bantam.

Diehl, Claudia, and Matthias Koenig. 2013. God Can Wait: New Migrants in Germany between Early Adaptation and Religious Reorganisation. *International Migration* 51(3): 8-22.

Dietz, Gunther. 2010. Frontier Hybridisation or Culture Clash? Transnational Migrant Communities and Subnational Identity Politics in Andalusia, Spain. *Journal of Ethnic and Migration Studies* 30 (6): 1087–1112.

Dietz, Gunther, and Nadia El-Shouhoumi. 2002. Door-to-Door with our Muslim Sisters: Intercultural and Interreligious Conflicts in Granada, Spain. *Migration Studies* 39:77–105.

Dolan, Jay P. 1972. Immigrants in the City: New York's Irish and German Catholics. *Church History* 41 (3): 354–68.

Dusenbery, Verne A. 1992. The Word as Guru: Sikh Scripture and the Translation Controversy. *History of Religions* 31 (4): 385–402.

Ebaugh, Helen Rose, and Janet Chafetz, eds. 2000. *Religion and the New Immigrants: Continuities and Adaptations in Immigrant Congregations*. Walnut Creek, CA: AltaMira.

Eisen, Arnold. 2009. Choosing Chosenness in America: The Changing Faces of Judaism. In *Immigration and Religion in America: Comparative and Historical Perspectives*, edited by R. Alba, A. J. Raborteau, and J. DeWind. New York: New York University Press.

Fetzer, Joel S., and J. Christopher Soper. 2005. *Muslims and the State in Britain, France, and Germany*. Cambridge: Cambridge University Press.

Finke, Roger, and Rodney Stark. 1992. *The Churching of America, 1776–2005: Winners and Losers in Our Religious Economy*. New Brunswick, NJ: Rutgers University Press.

Foley, Michael, and Dean R. Hoge. 2007. *Religion and the New Immigrants: How Faith Communities Form Our Newest Citizens*. New York: Oxford University Press.

Foner, Nancy, and Richard Alba. 2008. Immigrant Religion in the U.S. and Western Europe: Bridge or Barrier to Inclusion? *International Migration Review* 42 (2): 360–92.

Gans, Herbert J. 1999. Toward a Reconciliation of "Assimilation" and "Pluralism": The Interplay of Acculturation and Ethnic Retention. In *The Handbook of International Migration: The American Experience*, edited by C. Hirschman, P. Kasinitz, and J. DeWind. New York: Russell Sage Foundation.

George, Sheba. 1998. Caroling with the Keralites: The Negotiation of Gendered Space in an Indian Immigrant Church. In *Gatherings in Diaspora: Religious Communities and the New Immigrants*, edited by R. S. Warner and J. G. Wittner. Philadelphia: Temple University Press.

———. 2005. *When Women Come First: Gender and Class in Transnational Migration*. Berkeley, CA: University of California Press.

Gibb, Camilla, and Celia Rothenberg. 2000. Believeing Women: Harari and Palestinian Women at Home and in the Canadian Diaspora. *Journal of Muslim and Minority Affairs* 20:243–59.

Glazer, Nathan. 1993. Is Assimilation Dead? *Annals of the American Academy of Political and Social Science* 530:122–36.

———. 1997. *We Are All Multiculturalists Now.* Cambridge, MA: Harvard University Press.

Gordon, Milton. 1964. *Assimilation in American Life: The Role of Race, Religion, and National Origins.* New York: Oxford University Press.

Gorski, Philip S. 2003. *The Disciplinary Revolution: Calvinism and the Rise of the State in Early Modern Europe.* Chicago: University of Chicago Press.

Gozdziak, Elzbieta M. 2002. Spiritual Emergency Room: The Role of Spirituality and Religion in the Resettlement of Kosovar Albanians. *Journal of Refugee Studies* 15 (2): 136–52.

Guest, Kenneth. 2003. *God in Chinatown: Religion and Survival in New York's Evolving Immigrant Community.* New York: New York University Press.

Hagan, Jacqueline Maria. 2008. *Migration Miracle: Faith, Hope, and the Undocumented Journey.* Cambridge, MA: Harvard University Press.

Handlin, Oscar. 1973 [1951]. *The Uprooted: The Epic Story of the Great Migrations That Made the American People.* Boston: Little, Brown.

Harker, Kathryn. 2001. Immigrant Generation, Assimilation, and Adolescent Psychological Well-Being. *Social Forces* 79 (3): 969–1004.

Heath, Anthony, Catherine Rothon, and Elina Kilpi. 2008. The Second Generation in Western Europe: Education, Unemployment, and Occupational Attainment. *Annual Review of Sociology* 34:211–35.

Herberg, Will. 1960. *Protestant-Catholic-Jew.* Garden City, NY: Anchor Books.

Higham, John. 2007 [1955]. *Strangers in the Land: Patterns of American Nativism, 1860–1925.* New Brunswick, NJ: Rutgers University Press.

Hirschman, Charles. 2004. The Role of Religion in the Origins and Adaptation of Immigrant Groups in the United States. *International Migration Review* 28 (3): 1206–34.

Jacob, Konstanze, and Frank Kalter. 2013. Intergenerational Change in Religious Salience among Immigrant Families in Four European Countries. *International Migration* 51 (3): 38–56.

Kasinitz, Philip, John H. Mollenkopf, Mary C. Waters, and Jennifer Holdaway, eds. 2008. *Inheriting the City: The Children of Immigrants Come of Age.* New York: Russell Sage Foundation.

Kniss, Fred, and Paul D. Numrich. 2007. *Sacred Assemblies and Civic Engagement.* New Brunswick, NJ: Rutgers University Press.

Koenig, Matthias, and Phillip Connor. 2013. Explaining the Muslim Employment Gap: Individual Differences between Muslims and Non-Muslims in Western Europe. Paper read at Society for the Scientific Study of Religion, at Boston, MA.

Koopmans, Ruud. 2013. Multiculturalism and Immigration: A Contested Field in Cross-National Comparison. *Annual Review of Sociology* 39:147-69.

Koussens, David. 2009. Neutrality of the State and Regulation of Religious Symbols in Schools in Quebec and France. *Social Compass* 56:202–13.

Kurien, Prema. 2001. Religion, Ethnicity, and Politics: Hindu and Muslim Indian Immigrants in the United States. *Ethnic and Racial Studies* 24:263–93.

———. 2002. We Are Better Hindus Here. In *Religion in Asian America: Building Faith Communities*, edited by P. G. Min and J. H. Kim. Walnut Creek, CA: AltaMira.

Levitt, Peggy. 2007. *God Needs No Passport: Immigrants and the Changing American Religious Landscape*. New York: New Press.

Lewis, Valerie A., and Ridhi Kashyap. 2013. Piety in a Secular Society: Migration, Religiosity, and Islam in Britain. *International Migration* 51 (3): 57–66.

Lyon, David, and Marguerite Van Die, eds. 2000. *Rethinking Church, State, and Modernity*. Toronto: University of Toronto Press.

Massey, Douglas S., Joaquin Arango, Graeme Hugo, Ali Kouaouchi, Adela Pellegrimo, and J. Edward Taylor. 1998. *Worlds in Motion: Understanding International Migration at the End of the Millennium*. Oxford: Oxford University Press.

Meyer, Scott M. 2000. The Impact of Religious Involvement on Migration. *Social Forces* 79 (2): 755–73.

Min, Pyong Gap. 2010. *Preserving Ethnicity through Religion in America*. New York: New York University Press.

Mooney, Margarita. 2009. *Faith Makes Us Live: Surviving and Thriving in the Haitian Diaspora*. Berkeley: University of California Press.

Mullins, Mark. 1987. The Life-Cycle of Ethnic Churches in Sociological Perspective. *Japanese Journal of Religous Studies* 14 (4): 321–34.

Norris, Pippa. 2005. *Radical Right*. Cambridge: Cambridge University Press.

Norris, Pippa, and Ron Inglehart. 2004. *Sacred and Secular: Religion and Politics Worldwide*. Cambridge: Cambridge University Press.

Orsi, Robert, and Richard Alba. 2009. Passages in Piety: General Transitions and the Social and Religious Incorporation of Italian Americans. In *Immigration and Religion in America: Comparative and Historical Perspectives*, edited by R. Alba, A. Raboteau, and J. DeWind. New York: New York University Press.

O'Toole, Roger. 1996. Religion in Canada: Its Development and Contemporary Situation. *Social Compass* 43 (1): 119-34.

Park, Julie J. 2012. It Takes a Village (or an Ethnic Economy): The Varying Roles of Socioeconomic Status, Religion, and Social Capital in SAT Preparation for Chinese and Korean American Students. *American Educational Research Journal* 49 (4): 624–50.

Park, Robert Ezra, and Ernest W. Burgess. 1921 [1969]. *Introduction to the Science of Sociology*. Chicago: Chicago University Press.

Pedersen, Jon, and Kristen Dalen. 2007. Iraqis in Jordan: Their Number and Characteristics. Oslo, Norway: FAFO.

Pew Research Center. 2010. *Muslim Networks and Movements in Western Europe.* Washington, DC: Pew Research Center's Religion & Public Life Project.

———. 2011. *The Future of the Global Muslim Population: Projections for 2010–2030.* Washington, DC: Pew Research Center's Religion & Public Life Project.

———. 2012. *Faith on the Move: The Religious Affiliation of International Migrants.* Washington, DC: Pew Research Center's Religion & Public Life Project.

Portes, Alejandro. 2000. The Two Meanings of Social Capital. *Sociological Forum* 15 (1): 1–12.

Portes, Alejandro, and Ruben G. Rumbaut. 2001. *Legacies.* Berkeley: University of California Press.

———. 2006. *Immigrant America: A Portrait,* 3rd edition. Berkeley: University California Press.

Portes, Alejandro, and Erik Vickstom. 2011. Diversity, Social Capital, and Cohesion. *Annual Review of Sociology* 37:461–79.

Putnam, Robert. 2000. *Bowling Alone.* New York: Simon & Schuster.

———. 2007. E Pluribus Unum: Diversity and Community in the Twenty-first Century. The 2006 Johan Skytte Prize Lecture. *Scandinavian Political Studies* 30 (2): 137–74.

Putnam, Robert, and David E. Campbell. 2010. *American Grace: How Religion Divides and Unites Us.* New York: Simon & Schuster.

Reitz, Jeffrey G., Rupa Banerjee, Mai Phan, and Jordan Thompson. 2009. Race, Religion, and the Social Integration of New Immigrant Minorities in Canada. *International Migration Review* 43:695–726.

Skirbekk, Vegard, Eric Caron Malenfant, Stuart Basten, and Marcin Stonawski. 2012. The Religious Composition of the Chinese Diaspora, Focusing on Canada. *Journal for the Scientific Study of Religion* 51 (1): 173–83.

Smith, Christian, and Michael Emerson. 1998. *American Evangelicalism: Embattled and Thriving.* Chicago: University of Chicago Press.

Smith, Christian, David Sikink, and Jason Bailey. 1998. Devotion in Dixie and Beyond: A Test of the "Shibley Thesis" on the Effects of Regional Origin and Migration on Individual Religiosity. *Journal for the Scientific Study of Religion* 37 (3): 494–506.

Smith, Timothy L. 1978. Religion and Ethnicity in America. *American Historical Review* 83:1115–85.

Stephen, Elizabeth Hervey, and Frank D. Bean. 1992. Assimilation, Disruption, and the Fertility of Mexican-Origin Women in the United States. *International Migration Review* 26 (1): 67–88.

Telles, Edward Eric, and Vilma Ortiz. 2008. *Generations of Exclusion.* New York: Russell Sage Foundation.

Thomas, William I., and Florian Znaniecki, eds. 1996. *The Polish Peasant in Europe and America.* Urbana: University of Illinois Press.

Tilly, Charles. 1990. *Coercion, Capital, and European States, AD 990–1990.* Cambridge, MA: Blackwell.

Van Tubergen, Frank 2007. Religious Affiliation and Participation among Immigrants in a Secular Society: A Study of Immigrants in The Netherlands. *Journal of Ethnic and Migration Studies* 33 (5): 747–65.

———. 2013. Religious Change of New Immigrants in the Netherlands: The Event of Migration. *Social Science Research* 42:715–25.

Voas, David, and Fenella Fleischmann. 2012. Islam Moves West: Religious Change in the First and Second Generation. *Annual Review of Sociology* 38:525-45.

Warner, R. Stephen. 1994. The Place of the Congregation in the American Religious Configuration. In *New Perspectives in the Study of Congregations*, edited by J. P. Wind and J. W. Lewis. Chicago: University of Chicago Press.

———. 2007. The Role of Religion in the Process of Segmented Assimilation. *The Annals of the American Academy of Political and Social Science* 612:102–14.

Warner, R. Steven, and Judith G. Wittner, eds. 1998. *Gatherings in Diaspora: Religious Communities and the New Immigration*. Philadelphia: Temple University Press.

Wuthow, Robert, and Kevin Christiano. 1979. The Effects of Residential Migration on Church Attendance in the United States. In *The Religious Dimension: New Directions in Quantitative Research*, edited by R. Wuthnow. New York: Academic Press.

Yang, Fenggang. 1999. *Chinese Christians in America: Conversion, Assimilation, and Adhesive Identities*. University Park: Pennsylvania State University Press.

Yang, Fenggang, and Helen Rose Ebaugh. 2001. Religion and Ethnicity among New Immigrants: The Impact of Majority/Minority Status in Home and Host Countries. *Journal for the Scientific Study of Religion* 40 (3): 367–78.

Zolberg, Aristide R., and Long Litt Woon. 1999. Why Islam Is Like Spanish: Cultural Incorporation in Europe and the United States. *Politics and Society* 27 (1): 5–38.

INDEX

ABOUT THE AUTHOR

Phillip Connor is a Research Associate at the Pew Research Center's Religion & Public Life Project, where he researches the topics of immigration and religion worldwide. Prior to joining the Pew Research Center, Connor received his doctorate in sociology at Princeton University. His research has been published in leading academic journals and newspapers.